The Isles of Shoals

A Visual History

(Above) A panoramic view of Star Island and the first Oceanic Hotel. (Below) The steamboat Sightseer *at the Star Island dock. The second Oceanic Hotel dominates the skyline. Courtesy of UNH Media Services.*

The Isles of Shoals

A Visual History

John D. Bardwell

The Portsmouth Marine Society
Publication Fourteen

Published for the Society by

Peter E. Randall
PUBLISHER

Printed in the United States of America

Produced by
Peter E. Randall Publisher
Box 4726, Portsmouth, NH 03801

The Portsmouth Marine Society
Box 147, Portsmouth, NH 03801

Half Title Page—The first Oceanic Hotel on Star Island was built in 1873. It burned in 1875. Engraving by John A. Lowell. Courtesy of the Star Island Corporation.

Library of Congress Cataloging-in-Publication Data
Bardwell, John D.
The Isles of Shoals: a visual history / John D. Bardwell.
p. cm. -- (Publication / The Portsmouth Marine Society ; 14)
Includes bibliographical references.
ISBN 0-915819-13-9 : $35.00
1. Isles of Shoals (Me. and N.H.)--History--Pictorial works.
2. Isles of Shoals (Me. and N.H.)--Description and travel--Views.
I. Portsmouth Marine Society. II. Title. III. Series; Publication (Portsmouth Marine Society) ; 14.
F42.I8B37 1989
974.2'6'00222--dc20

Other Portsmouth Marine Society Publications:

1. *John Haley Bellamy, Carver of Eagles*
2. *The Prescott Story*
3. *The Piscataqua Gundalow, Workhorse for a Tidal Basin Empire*
4. *The Checkered Career of Tobias Lear*
5. *Clippers of the Port of Portsmouth and the Men Who Built Them*
6. *Portsmouth-Built Submarines of the Portsmouth Naval Shipyard*
7. *Atlantic Heights, A World War I Shipbuilders' Community*
8. *There Are No Victors Here*
   A Local Perspective on the Treaty of Portsmouth
9. *The Diary of the Portsmouth, Kittery and York Electric Railroad*
10. *Port of Portsmouth Ships and the Cotton Trade*
11. *Port of Dover, Two Centuries of Shipping on the Cochecho*
12. *Wealth and Honour*
    Portsmouth During the Golden Age of Privateering, 1775-1815
13. *The Sarah Mildred Long Bridge*
    A History of the Maine-New Hampshire Interstate
    Bridge from Portsmouth, New Hampshire, to Kittery, Maine

To my wife, Anne Bardwell, for her support and understanding. When my reading area becomes completely surrounded by books, when all shopping trips have to include a bookstore, when most of the bills are for computer supplies and when indexing tests my patience, she finds a way to explain my behavior to family and friends. That is what is meant by support and understanding.

Boats at anchor in Gosport harbor with Smuttynose Island in the background. Courtesy of UNH Media Services.

Other Publications by John D. Bardwell

The Diary of the Portsmouth, Kittery and York Electric Railroad (1986)

A History of the Country Club at York, Maine (1988)

Publications by John D. Bardwell and Ronald P. Bergeron

Images of a University: A Photographic History of the University of New Hampshire (1984)

The White Mountains of New Hampshire: A Visual History (1989)

The Lakes Region of New Hampshire: A Visual History (1989)

Acknowledgments

THIS HISTORY OF THE ISLES OF SHOALS is an attempt to share some of the magic that I feel when I am involved with these special islands and those who love them. To prepare such a publication requires the support of many people who share their knowledge and resources with the author of the book. I would like to acknowledge the contributions of the Star Island Corporation, the Portsmouth Naval Shipyard, the Portsmouth Public Library, the New Hampshire Historical Society, the Maine Historic Preservation Commission, the Rye Historical Society, the Star Island Museum, UNH Special Collections and UNH Media Services.

The people who shared were Louise H. Tallman of the Rye Historical Society, Robert L. Bradley of the Maine Historic Preservation Commission, John Hutchinson, who shared an album of old photographs, George A. Sylvester, a photographer who documents life at the Shoals Marine Laboratory, author William Varrell, Rosamond Thaxter, who shared stories and pictures, Gary Samson, a filmmaker and photographer, Dr. John B. Heiser, Director, Shoals Marine Laboratory, and Fred McGill, the venerated historian who has shared the island traditions with so many people. Robert Tuttle, a colleague who shares my interest in the islands, was kind enough to read the manuscript to identify both real and tactical errors.

The research for this book began many years before I realized that it was happening. During that period, there were many people who added to my mental files and shaped the stories that appear on these pages. In some ways the book is an expression of thanks for their interest in me and my love for the Isles of Shoals.

JDB

Contents

(Above) An early photograph of the White Island lighthouse from an original stereoview by William Hobbs of Exeter, NH. Courtesy of the Portsmouth Public Library. (Below) White Island lighthouse and Coast Guard station as it appeared in 1977. Photo by John D. Bardwell.

Introduction

THE ISLES OF SHOALS ARE NINE BARREN ISLANDS off the coast of Maine and New Hampshire that were the site of one of the very first settlements in America. A popular Victorian summer resort, the islands have been the home of several ghosts, a source of buried treasure, the scene of several shipwrecks and a cold blooded murder. Archaeologist Faith Harrington has written that the Isles of Shoals have been a crucial resource as long as Europeans have inhabited the new world. It was the Europeans' off-shore fishing that led to the clustering of populations in coastal areas and the establishment of vital trade links between New England and Europe.

The islands lie in two states. Duck Island; Appledore, originally called Hog Island; Smuttynose or Haley's; Malaga, a tiny pile of rocks; and Cedar belong to Maine. White and Seavey's, separated at high tide; Lunging or Londoners; and Star are in New Hampshire. Star was formerly known as Gosport, a fishing village with records that go back to 1731. Some writers attribute the name to the shoals, or schools, of fish that were seen along the coast at certain seasons of the year. However, east of the islands is an extensive shoal called Jeffrey's Ledge which was a popular fishing ground for the islanders. This reef appears on the early charts and navigators would pass through the area very carefully with the islands, the shoals and Mount Agamenticus as important marks to help them find their way. In addition there are nine rocks or ledges, many of which would cause the water to break over them in a threatening manner. Jimmie's Ledge, Eastern Rock and Mingo Rock surround Duck Island. Old Henry, Cedar Ledge, and Anderson circle outside Appledore, Cedar and Star. White Ledge is close to White Island, Square Rock is near Lunging Island and Halfway Rocks are between Lunging and Star. The Isles of Shoals would be a type of descriptive name that

(Above) Appledore fishermen with their nets in an open boat were a common sight around the islands. Courtesy of John Hutchinson. (Right) A map of the Isles of Shoals showing the islands, rocks, and ledges. The big island is still named Hog Island on this map so it was probably prepared before Thomas Laighton decided that it should be called Appledore, the name applied to the entire settlement in the 1600s. Courtesy of the Rye Historical Society.

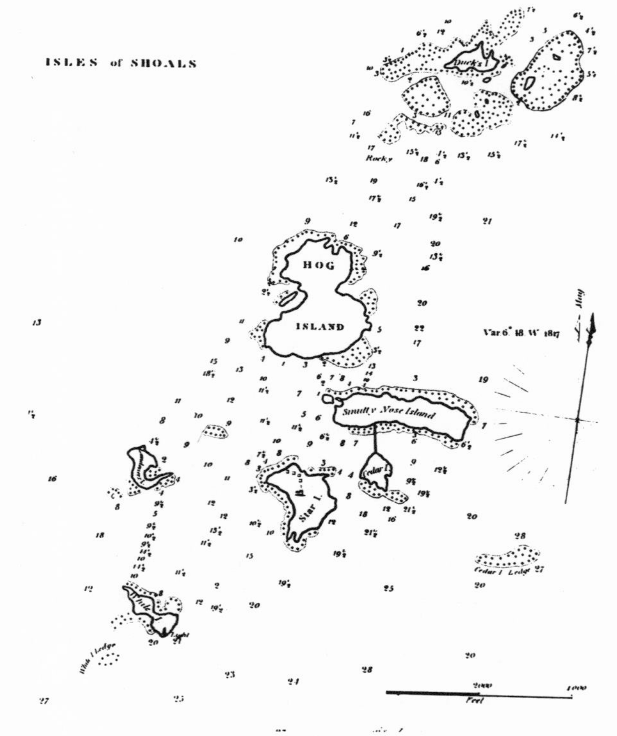

would have been acceptable to early fishermen who passed on information by word-of-mouth.

A major cod fishing industry had become established by 1620 and it continued well into the nineteenth century. During the eighteenth century, the price of fish on the world market was quoted from the Isles of Shoals. The climate allowed large cod to be cured to a golden brown with the use of very little salt. The product, called "Dunfish" was one of the more important products in New England's economy. It is recorded that in 1822, dunfish from the Shoals sold for $8 per hundred pounds while the other dried fish sold for $2.40.

Fish drying racks or "flakes" near the Hontvet house on Smuttynose. From a stereograph by the Davis Brothers. Courtesy of the Star Island Corporation.

Curing Fish

The process of curing, or, as the islanders called it, "saving," fish did not change in two hundred years. The fish were thrown from the boat and piled up on the shore. The "cutter" took each fish, cut its throat and slit open its belly. He passed it to the "header" who removed the entrails and the liver and broke off the heads. The "splitter" removed the backbone, split the fish completely open, and handed it to the "salter." The fish were salted and piled in bulk where they remained for ten to twenty hours. When convenient, the shoremen and women washed them and spread them on drying racks called flakes. Curing could take three or four weeks, depending on the weather. During this time they were often turned, piled in fagots, and then spread out again until they were completely cured.

The "dun" or winter fish were larger and thicker than the summer fish. They were cured in cold weather with very little salt and were transparent when held up to the light. These fish sometimes weighed a hundred pounds or more and great pains were taken in drying them. The women sometimes covered the fagots with bed quilts to keep them clean. Dunfish were highly prized in Spain and the Mediterranean ports, bringing the highest price during Lent.

(Above) The Appledore Hotel complex as it appeared from Celia's cottage. The tennis courts are in the foreground. Courtesy of UNH Media Services.

In addition to being one of the first settlements in America, the Isles of Shoals were also one of the most popular summer resorts. Samuel Haley's Mid-Ocean House on Smuttynose was purchased by Thomas Laighton when he acquired Hog, Smuttynose, and Malaga Islands in 1839. Mrs. Laighton apparently established a good business with people who found the island to be a charming vacation site. When Thomas Laighton failed to receive a postmaster's appointment, he moved his family to Hog Island, renamed it Appledore, and established what eventually became a fashionable and popular summer resort.

Thomas Laighton's three children, Celia, Oscar, and Cedric, made Appledore famous during the last half of the century. Cedric and Oscar took over the hotel from their father, purchased the Oceanic Hotel on Star Island, and became the innkeepers for the Isles of Shoals. Celia became one of New England's most popular authors and attracted writers, painters and musicians to the Shoals. Through her, the influence of the Shoals touched notables from all walks of life.

Thomas H. Elliott, a Unitarian layman, visited the islands with his wife in 1896 instead of attending a Unitarian Assembly at the Weirs on Lake Winnipesaukee. Mrs. Elliott found the ocean breezes much more pleasant than the sweltering inland temperatures and her husband discovered that the two hotels needed patrons. He began a letter writing

(Left) John Greenleaf Whittier was a great admirer of Celia Thaxter and they corresponded regularly. (Right) John Weiss came to the Mid-Ocean House as a young man and returned to the Shoals for many years. He brought his friend Levi Thaxter who became a tutor for the Laighton children and a partner in the Appledore Hotel. Courtesy of UNH Media Services.

campaign that succeeded in filling all the rooms in the two hotels for a week in July, 1897. The meetings were successful and the program grew over the years. The Appledore Hotel burned after the season of 1914 and the Oceanic was about to be sold. In 1915, Lewis Parkhurst bought Star Island for $16,000 and held it until the Star Island Corporation could get organized and raise enough money to purchase the property. The programs were basically designed for church people who wanted to enrich their lives spiritually, intellectually, and emotionally.

In 1924, the Star Island Corporation bought the Appledore Hotel reservation and five years later acquired the remaining vacant land on Appledore, giving them control of 95% of the island. In 1928, the University of New Hampshire leased three of the buildings for a marine zoological laboratory and summer "camp" under the direction of Professor C. Floyd Jackson. The reputation of the program attracted students from many colleges and universities, but the lease was not renewed in 1938 and as a result of World War II the islands were turned into a military base. In 1966, Doctor John Kingsbury of Cornell University, with the encouragement of the Star Island Corporation, offered a course in marine science before the regular conference season

continued on page 9

(Above) Another boathouse near the Laighton cottage with lobster pots, oars and rubber boots. Courtesy of the Star Island Corporation. (Below) The Pink Parlor at the Oceanic Hotel as it appeared in 1924. Courtesy of UNH Media Services.

ISLES OF SHOALS

OFF

PORTSMOUTH, N. H.

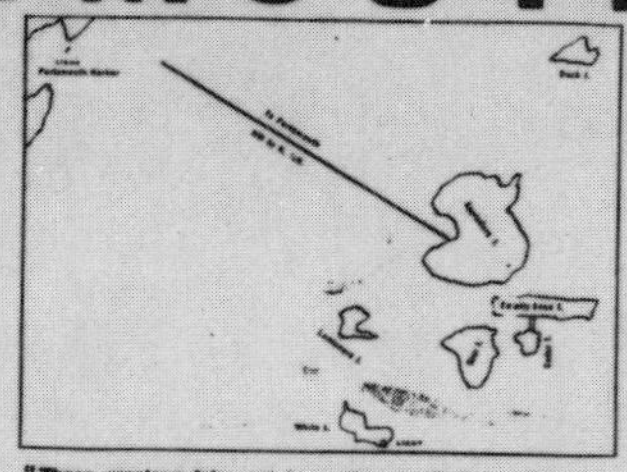

"These precious isles set in a silver sea."—CELIA THAXTER.

AN IDEAL SUMMER RESORT OF THE HIGHEST CLASS

AND FULL OF HISTORIC ASSOCIATIONS.

PRE-EMINENTLY THE PLACE FOR THE TIRED WORKER.

NO NOISE. NO DUST. NO TROLLEYS. A REST CURE IN THESE ISLES IS A THING OF JOY. THE CLIMATE IS PERFECT. THE SUNSETS GLORIOUS. HIGHEST SHADE TEMPERATURE, 75; AVERAGE, 65 AT NOON.

THE HOTEL OPENS THE LAST WEEK IN JUNE

AND CLOSES ABOUT THE 10th OF SEPTEMBER.

SEPTEMBER IS AN IDEAL MONTH AND GUESTS SATISFIED WITH A PLAIN TABLE AFTER 10th SEPTEMBER CAN BE ACCOMMODATED BY SPECIAL ARRANGEMENT UNTIL THE END OF THE MONTH.

THIS IS A GREAT RESORT FOR ANYONE SUFFERING FROM

INSOMNIA, HAYFEVER, OR ROSECOLD.

MANY GUESTS HAVE BEEN VISITING THESE ISLANDS REGULARLY FOR 20, 30 AND 40 YEARS, AND ALL WHO GO THERE ONCE INVARIABLY RETURN.

FAMILIES DESIRING ABSOLUTE PRIVACY CAN RENT SOME OF THE COTTAGES WHICH ARE QUITE CLOSE TO THE HOTEL, WHILE STILL TAKING THEIR MEALS IN THE MAIN HOUSE.

TERMS: FROM 2½ DOLLARS AND UPWARD.

EXCELLENT TABLE.

A GOOD STEAMBOAT CONNECTS THE ISLANDS WITH THE MAINLAND, DISTANT ABOUT 7 MILES. THE MOST TIMID SAILORS CAN CHOOSE THEIR OWN DAY TO CROSS, REMAINING AT PORTSMOUTH TO SUIT THEIR CONVENIENCE.

PERFECTLY SAFE BATHING AND, OF COURSE, BOATING AND TENNIS.

A WIRELESS STATION CONNECTS THE ISLANDS WITH THE MAINLAND.

BOAT SERVICE THRICE DAILY, CONNECTING WITH PORTSMOUTH R.R. SERVICE.

A DOCTOR IS RESIDENT AT APPLEDORE ALL SEASON.

APPLEDORE HOUSE, Appledore Island,
OCEANIC HOUSE, Star Island, ...
LEIGHTON BROS., PROPRIETORS.

This 1898 broadside advertises the Isles of Shoals as a great resort for anyone suffering from insomnia, hayfever, or rosecold. Courtesy of the Portsmouth Public Library.

(Above) The University of New Hampshire research vessel Jere Chase *coming into the dock after a successful trip. (Right) A class in session at the Shoals Marine Laboratory in 1979. Courtesy of UNH Media Services.*

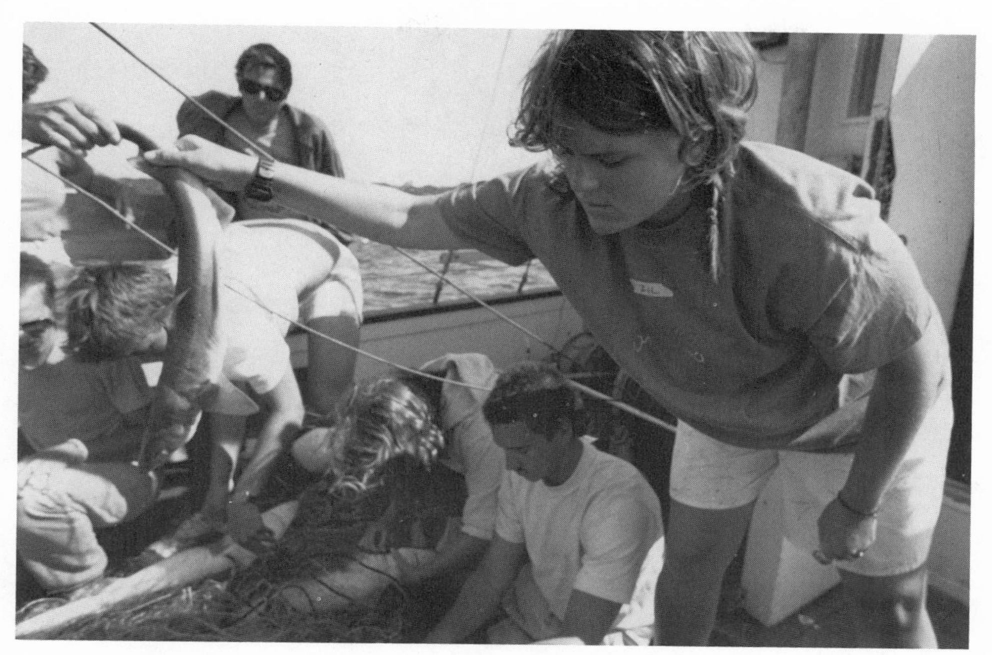

A student pulls a fish from the net on the UNH research vessel. Marine science students can expect to have plenty of "hands-on" action. Courtesy of UNH Media Services.

opened in June. By 1971, Dr. Kingsbury had the resources to negotiate a long-term lease of Appledore and begin the construction of the buildings required to house a marine laboratory. Classes moved to Appledore in 1973, and by 1979, the building program was essentially completed. There were 10 buildings, including three new dormitories and the Palmer-Kinne Laboratory with bench space for sixty students. Cornell and the University of New Hampshire now share responsibility for the course offerings. Faculty members are drawn from across the nation.

The original lighthouse and a cottage on White Island were built in 1820 and became the childhood home of Celia Thaxter, whose father was lighthouse keeper between 1839 and 1847. The lighthouse was a stone tower with a lantern approximately ninety feet above the water. Visitors to White Island during this period included Richard Henry Dana, author of *Two Years Before the Mast*, and novelist Nathaniel Hawthorne. In 1865, the light tower was entirely rebuilt of granite. The walls were constructed two feet thick, and the kitchen extended the full length of the house.

Cedar Island is the home of lobster fishermen and has maintained the tradition of the early fishing village. Six generations of Foyes and Halls have lived on the island during the summer and they supply

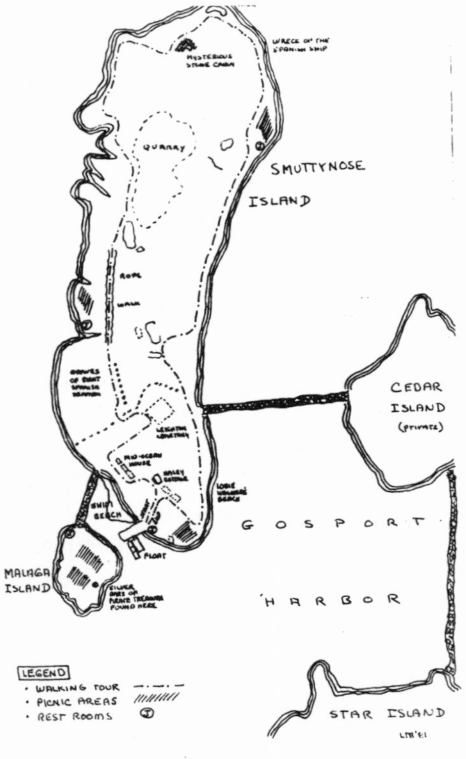

(Above) An early sketch of the buildings on White Island. Courtesy of the Portsmouth Public Library. (Left) A map showing the route for a walking tour of Smuttynose Island. Note that the Leighton (Laighton) cemetery is actually on Appledore. The Haley family is buried in the Smuttynose Cemetery.

A two-masted whaleboat being sailed along the shore of Appledore. Courtesy of the Star Island Corporation.

most of the lobsters served at the Star Island hotel. Of special interest is the "long house," a building that was once on Captain Haley's pier on Smuttynose Island. Like many buildings on the islands, it was moved many years ago. Four cottages on the southern tip of Appledore are still privately owned and used as summer quarters by families who fish for lobsters around the islands. Lunging Island is privately owned and features a small summer cottage.

A rock formation of the type that attracted artists and writers to the rugged islands. Courtesy of UNH Media Services.

In the Beginning

The Great Ice Age

THESE ISLANDS WERE PROBABLY PART of the mainland when the great ice cap spread slowly down from Canada tens of thousands of years ago. The entire area was covered with a sheet of ice, thousands of feet thick, which scraped away the soil, smoothed the ledges, rounded the hills, and created deep valleys. Huge boulders were pushed around under the ice or carried in the ice sheet.

The weight of the glacier caused the land to be depressed and the sea level was several hundred feet lower than at present. The water level was also lower because the ice cap was made up of water evaporated from the sea. As the ice sheet melted, the water was returned to the ocean, and the lowlands and valleys were flooded far inland. About 10,000 years ago, the Isles of Shoals, which had been hills in the lowlands, became islands. However, the evidence of the ice age still remains. For example, the "whale-backed" shape of the ledges suggests that the ice passed over the islands from northwest to southeast, leaving a smooth northwest side and a jagged southeast side. All of the original soil was removed by the scouring action of the ice sheet and the thin soil that now covers the islands is essentially made up of decayed vegetable matter or fragments of minerals that have eroded from the exposed rock surfaces.

The forces of erosion attacked the exposed surfaces of these rocky islands as soon as they emerged from the ice. The waves of winter storms rolled in from the northeast and southeast, forming steep cliffs on the eastern shores. Freezing and thawing opened small cracks, breaking down the rock surfaces. A few rocks still show the polished surface caused by the ice, but the surfaces subject to erosion are now rough and uneven.

Early geologists suggested that the hills and ridges were the summit of a high mountain surrounded by a rising sea fed by the waters from melting glaciers. We now know that each island is the base of a mountain

A postcard view of a basalt dike on the Isles of Shoals. Courtesy of the Portsmouth Public Library.

whose alpine peak was reduced by erosion and sheared off by the ice flow during the last ice age, ten thousand years ago.

Many islands off the Maine coast were densely wooded, but available historical records suggest that the Isles of Shoals had a vegetation of shrubs, with a few larger specimens that had been shaped by the wind. Captain John Smith described them as barren rocks, many overgrown with shrubs and sharp vines, without either grass of wood. He did mention three or four short, shrubby old cedars, from which Cedar Island may have derived its name.

Celia Thaxter felt that the islands may have been covered with spruce and cedar. On Smuttynose she found a root of cedarwood deep in the crevice of a rock. She had seen a few bushes with maple, poplar, and birch leaves that had been browsed down by the sheep. She had also seen the rotting stumps of large trees in the valley at Appledore. Critics suggest that Mrs. Thaxter was describing storm-tossed driftwood and, unfortunately, there is no way to check her observations.

Archaeological Studies

Probably first visited by Europeans in the seventeenth century and continuously occupied from the early second decade of that century, the islands are rich in archaeological remains. They have been virtually undisturbed since the nineteenth century and the waters around the islands abound with opportunities for marine archaeologists. In 1982, under the direction of Robert T. Farrell of Cornell University, work began on the remains of a vessel sunk near Duck Island. Timbers were raised for study and it was tentatively determined that the wreck was a small coastal schooner, built c. 1900.

David Yesner, of the University of Southern Maine, volunteered to support Farrell's work by conducting surveys on Appledore and Smuttynose. They found significant remains of early colonial occupation on both sites. A fragment of prehistoric pottery was found on Appledore which may indicate that Indians did occupy or visit the Shoals. Excavation in a stone-lined cellar hole revealed many artifacts that dated the site at approximately 1760. It may have functioned as a fisherman's dwelling, a storage building, or a fish drying hut.

In 1986, Faith Harrington conducted a four-day survey on Star Island to determine the extent and nature of the archaeological remains. The survey revealed intact structural remains of Fort Star which was built in 1653 to protect the fishermen from Indians and hostile ships. It was occupied until the residents were evacuated at the beginning of the Revolutionary War.

Oral tradition indicated that a trading post was built on Lunging Island by the London Company in the decade between 1620 and 1630. It was from this trading post that fish, furs and timber from the mainland were shipped to England, Europe and the West Indies in exchange for sugar, wine and manufactured goods. A stone foundation on the northeast end of the island had been identified as a possible site for this trading post. However, excavations in and around the supposed foundation yielded scanty evidence of an early seventeenth-century trading post. Many nineteenth-century artifacts were recovered which provided useful information about the construction dates of the two existing buildings on Lunging Island.

Building inventory research has identified over forty structures on Appledore, not including buildings associated with the early fishery. An important site is the reputed location of the house of William Pepperrell, a prosperous merchant who was actively involved in the fishing business. Aerial photographs, cartographic information, and other documents have been used to develop building inventories and map structural remains on each one of the islands. These inventories are being used to identify potential areas for future archaeological investigation.

Captain John Smith, Admiral of New England, who named the islands "Smith's Isles" and claimed them for himself. Smith realized that the rich fishing grounds were the most valuable economic resources of the area. Courtesy of the New Hampshire Historical Society.

Explorers, Fishermen and Early Settlers

The Early Explorers

WE ARE ACCUSTOMED TO BELIEVING that the coast of New England was virtually unknown until the arrival of the early explorers described in school textbooks. In reality, fleets of fishing vessels probably visited the eastern Atlantic annually during the entire sixteenth century. The "doggers" and "pinkes" of the English, the "busses" of Holland and Zealand, the "fly-boats" of Flanders, the "biskiner" and the "portingal" were all regular visitors to the fishing grounds. Although there has been no archaeological evidence of their presence, it is possible that some of them were based at the Isles of Shoals. In Captain Richard Whitbourne's report of his observations in Newfoundland he wrote, "More than four hundred sail of fishing ships were annually sent to the Grand Banks by the French and Portuguese, making two voyages a year, fishing winter and summer."

In 1615, Whitbourne reported two hundred and fifty ships off the coast of Newfoundland. He estimated that approximately five thousand men and boys were needed to crew those ships. De Poutrincourt, who was in Port Royal in 1618, estimated the fishery to be worth a "million d'or" annually to France. He also predicted that the English would threaten New France as soon as they had a strong foothold in Virginia.

Fishing near the Isles of Shoals had many advantages. There was deep water with a reasonably secure anchorage for the ships. Fishermen were free from attack by Indians while they were engaged in catching and curing the fish. Most important of all, they were near the best fishing grounds. Great quantities of fish could be caught in a very short period of time. The hooks hardly reached the bottom when a fish would bite. They would pull them in as fast as they could get the hooks back in the water. Cabot described cod by the name of "bacalo," Jean Alfonse speaks of "bacaillos," Captain Uring called them "baccalew" and the Indian name was "tamwock." According to Captain John Smith, fifteen or eighteen men hooked sixty thousand fish in a month.

On July 15, 1605, a French bark of fifteen tons was standing off the coast of New England, searching for a place to begin a settlement. Pierre du Guast, Sieur de Monts was the leader of the expedition and the geographer was Samuel Champlain. For a month they had been cruising the Maine coast hoping to find a more suitable place for habitation than the site of De Monts' little colony on the Isle of St. Croix. To the west was a deep bay which Indians identified as a river mouth. On the horizon they saw three or four islands of "fair" elevation. Historians agree that these were the Isles of Shoals. The detail of this journey along the New England coast in 1605 was the first intelligible record to be found.

Sir Samuel Argal in the *Discovery* and Sir George Somers in the *Patience* left Jamestown in 1610 to pick up provisions in the Bermudas. Their ships were blown off course and Argal spent the summer cruising and fishing up and down the coast of Maine. Accounts of that voyage indicate that the *Discovery* frequently made a harbor at the Isles of Shoals during the summer and returned to Virginia heavily freighted with fish. In 1613, Argal returned to the coast leading a convoy of ten or eleven fishing vessels.

Argal learned from the Indians that the French had established a settlement of Jesuits on Mount Desert, which was considered English territory. Argal attacked the settlement, destroyed the buildings, killed one of the priests, and made prisoners of the inhabitants. Later that summer, the Governor of Virginia ordered him back to Acadia where he destroyed the French settlements at St. Croix and Port Royal.

Fishermen

In 1614, Captain John Smith, in command of two London ships, visited the Isles of Shoals on a fishing and trading voyage. The objective was to take whales and search for copper and gold. If that didn't prove feasible, they were to settle for fish and furs. They chased whales but couldn't catch them and the search for minerals was unsuccessful. In the meantime, the crew fished and Smith ranged the coast trading for furs. Smith returned to England with his cargo. There he published an interesting account of this coast which identified "Smiths Isles" and "Accominticus" as the "remarkablest Isles and mountains for landmarks." The islands referred to were the present Isles of Shoals which the great navigator chose to perpetuate his name. A few years later, the patentees schemed to divide their territory into twenty parts and the Captain temporarily became Lord and Proprietor of the rocky, barren rocks off the coast of Maine and New Hampshire.

Captain John Smith's monument as it appeared in 1881. Only one "Turk's head" remains. Courtesy of the Portsmouth Public Library.

Christopher Levett is the first Englishman to give an account of the Isles of Shoals. He wrote,

> The first place I set foot upon in New England was the Isle of Shoals, being islands in the sea about two leagues from the main. Upon these islands I could see neither one good timber-tree nor so much good ground as to make a garden. The place is found to be a good fishing place for six ships, but more can not well be there, for want of convenient stage room, as this years experience hath proved.

The year was 1623, and this was the earliest record of the islands being occupied as a fishing station.

Each of the six vessels described by Levett carried at least fifty men. That meant three hundred fishermen were based on the islands. About one third of the men lived ashore to dry and cure the catch while the others cruised the coast searching for mackerel and cod. Shelters had to be constructed for approximately one hundred men, fishing stages were floating platforms projecting into the harbor, sheds were needed for splitting and salting the fish, and flakes along the rocks held the fish while they dried. At the time of Levett's visit the harbor was inconveniently crowded with stages indicating that a great deal of business was being conducted in that port. According to Smith, the codfish caught off the Isles of Shoals were larger than those caught off the banks of Newfoundland and the climate was excellent for the curing of fish for market. The fishermen introduced a process of drying and sweating without salt. This technique produced the famous "dunfish" which brought a high price in Europe.

Settlers

The year 1628, marks the first time that actual settlers can be documented on the Isles of Shoals. Mr. Jeffrey and Mr. Burslem, taverners at the Shoals, greeted Miles Standish that summer when he sailed into the harbor with Thomas Morton of Merrymount as his prisoner. Morton was reputed to have endangered the settlements by trading firearms with the Indians and was being sent back to England. The two men were presented a bill for two pounds to go toward the expense of deportation on the grounds that Morton was a menace to the colonies. Their names on that bill identify them as the first settlers at the Shoals whose names appear on any document.

The three Cutt brothers settled there in 1645, but they soon moved to the mainland. Antipas Maverick was a resident in 1647, William Pepperrell, father of the hero of Louisbourg, came in 1676, but moved to Kittery after a brief stay at the Shoals. Mrs. John Reynolds came to reside at Hog Island in defiance of a court order prohibiting women from living on the islands. In 1647, Richard Cutt petitioned for her removal along with the goats and swine that her husband permitted to run wild on the island. The court permitted her to remain, but Reynolds had twenty days to remove the animals. Society on the barren rocks must have been rather primitive because people of substance left for the mainland as soon as possible.

Sir Ferdinando Gorges and John Mason divided their holdings in the new world in 1635, but neither of them was willing to give up the profit in the Isles of Shoals. They divided them through Gosport Harbor. The southern islands, including Star, Londoners, Seavey's and White went to Mason and New Hampshire. The northern part, with Hog, Smuttynose, Cedar, Malaga, and Duck, went to Gorges and Maine. Massachusetts annexed Maine in 1652, and the Shoalers wasted little time in petitioning for more self-determination by establishing Appledore township to include all of the islands, whether in Maine or New Hampshire. Their first two petitions were rejected but, in 1661, they became a town on the third try. The township was dissolved in 1682

continued on page 25

Sir William Pepperrell, son of Colonel William Pepperrell who was a resident of the Isles of Shoals in 1676. The elder Pepperrell was engaged in the fishing business which provided the foundation for his family's fortune. From the author's collection.

Hon. Wm. Pepperrell

According to tradition, William Pepperrell's home was located on the north slope on a knoll on Appledore Island. The location once had a small marker which read:

The
Island Home
of
Hon. Wm. Pepperrell
Maine Historical Society 1900

From his house, Pepperrell could see the mainland which was eight miles away. The view includes a small cove in Kittery that came to be called Pepperrell's Cove. William probably selected this island location because the terrain was suitable for drying and salting fish. He had come from an English village which subsisted mainly by fishing, and he engaged in fishing on the Isles of Shoals from the time he came from England in 1676 until 1680. The business became the foundation for the family fortune which was enhanced when he married the daughter of prosperous shipbuilder John Bray.

William Pepperrell and his son, also William, became involved in shipping, sending their vessels across the Atlantic, the Caribbean, the North Sea, and the Mediterranean. Their ships carried rum, sugar, molasses, passengers, lumber, naval stores, and foreign fruits. They were considered to be the most important mercantile firm in colonial America.

Sir William Pepperrell commanded English regiments at the capture of Louisbourg and for this service was created a baronet by King George II on November 15, 1746. He inherited his father's home in Kittery Point which he expanded and redecorated.

At one time there were enough people on Star Island to require the operation of a one-room schoolhouse. Courtesy of the Portsmouth Public Library.

Gosport Architecture

According to Lyman Rutledge, noted Isles of Shoals historian, the houses in Gosport were very similar in size and design. The small structures had two rooms divided by a stairway on the first floor, and two rooms above. The entire house was built on a 15-by-30-foot foundation so the rooms were approximately 15 by 15. The only heat came from small fireplaces and sometimes the entire family would live in one room.

The barren islands offered little protection from the howling winter winds and the residents spent most of the winter indoors. They would seal the windows and doors as tight as possible. An entire family would live in one little room along with fishing boots, beds, furniture, cook stove or fireplace, oil lamp, and tobacco-pipes smoked by both sexes.

It is easy to understand why they suffered so much from ill health and why so many died from consumption. Their lived in an area where the air was almost perfect in its purity, but they created living conditions that poisoned them with every breath.

(Above) An early view of Star Island taken from a stereoview by the Davis Brothers of Portsmouth. The school is at center, the parsonage at left. Courtesy of the Star Island Corporation. (Below, left) View of the meetinghouse when it had a wooden tower. C. 1881. From the album of Rev. Charles E. Dunn. Courtesy of the Star Island Corporation. (Below, right) Lyman Rutledge, Isles of Shoals historian and author of The Isles of Shoals in Lore and Legend, *entertaining five of his friends on the Star Island dock. Photo by Clifton Follansbee. Courtesy of the Portsmouth Public Library.*

(Above) A fanciful illustration of "Gorges and Mason naming their provinces." They were as concerned about the division of the Isles of Shoals as they were about their holdings on the mainland. Courtesy of the New Hampshire Historical Society. (Below) "Betty Moody's Hole" among the rocky ledges on Star Island. Courtesy of the Portsmouth Public Library.

and the Council of New Hampshire reported that the Shoals were not under any government at all. This suited the independent Shoalers who ignored a court order to build a meetinghouse on the northern islands, ignored an order to appoint a Representative to sit in the General Assembly, failed to attend elections, and failed to pay taxes.

Most of the Shoalers were living on Hog and Smuttynose at the time and they were subject to Massachusetts taxes which they considered unfair. Land was available on Star Island which belonged to New Hampshire so the islanders became involved in a mass migration to Star Island. Their homes and the old church on Smuttynose were abandoned. A meetinghouse with a tower and bell was built on the highest point on Star, the site of the present meetinghouse. In 1715, The New Hampshire Provincial Assembly made Star Island a township named Gosport.

There were only a couple of occasions when the Shoals residents had to worry about attacks by the French and Indians. In 1691, a large body of eastern Indians came down the Maine coast with the intention of attacking the islands. They were intercepted by English forces under Captain March and were unable to carry out their plan. In 1692, three deserters from Canada reported that two French vessels were being outfitted to attack Wells, the Shoals, and the Piscataqua region. This plan was also thwarted. In 1653, the Shoalers had erected a rough stone fort on the western hill of Star Island overlooking the harbor. However, by 1692, the stones were scattered and the guns were buried in the rubble. The not-so-independent Shoalers petitioned the government to send 40 soldiers under competent officers to rebuild the fort. They agreed that food, shelter, and wages would be provided for forty men, but when Captain Willy arrived, the three largest absentee landlords ordered their tenants, employees, and servants not to support the project. Captain Willy kept his men at the island for a full month while they constructed a fort that was 50-feet square. They reconditioned the two guns and nine four-pounders were added. The islanders paid what they could and the Province was responsible for the deficit. The only account of an Indian raid was during Lovewell's War in 1724. The Indians came down the coast in fifty canoes and terrorized all the settlements. They captured twenty-two vessels, including one armed with swivel-guns, and sailed to attack the Isles of Shoals. The Shoalers manned the old fort on Star Island and most of the village must have been assembled there. The Indians cut out two shallops and left. Betty Moody, in panic, hid with her small children in a small cave on the island. Her baby began to cry and she covered its mouth with her hand. When the danger was over she discovered to her horror that the baby had smothered.

Reverend John Tucke was called to the Isles of Shoals in 1731. He

continued on page 29

(Above) Smuttynose Island as it appeared in 1870. Left to right are the Mid-Ocean House, the Samuel Haley house, the Hontvet house, the warehouses and the pier. The photograph was taken from Malaga Island. (Below) Fishing and lobstering gear are scattered along the island shore. Courtesy of the Star Island Corporation.

A Walking Tour of Gosport

In front of the fishhouses were tubs of trawls, a barrel or two of fish oil, a pile of split fish, and a half hogshead in which split fish had just been salted down. There was a wheelbarrow, used to carry fish from the boat, a lobster pot, and a pair of rusty scales. Sou'westers and suits of oilskin clothing decorated the walls of the fishhouses. In the loft was a collection of oars, no two of the same length.

Whaleboats, hauled out to be caulked and painted, were in some of the boathouses. They were schooner-rigged and some were decked over to provide shelter in bad weather. These very seaworthy craft usually contained a coil of half-inch line and a brace of powder kegs for trawls.

This sign describing the history of Fort Star was found under the summer house and photographed by Emily Bush in 1921. Courtesy of the Star Island Corporation.

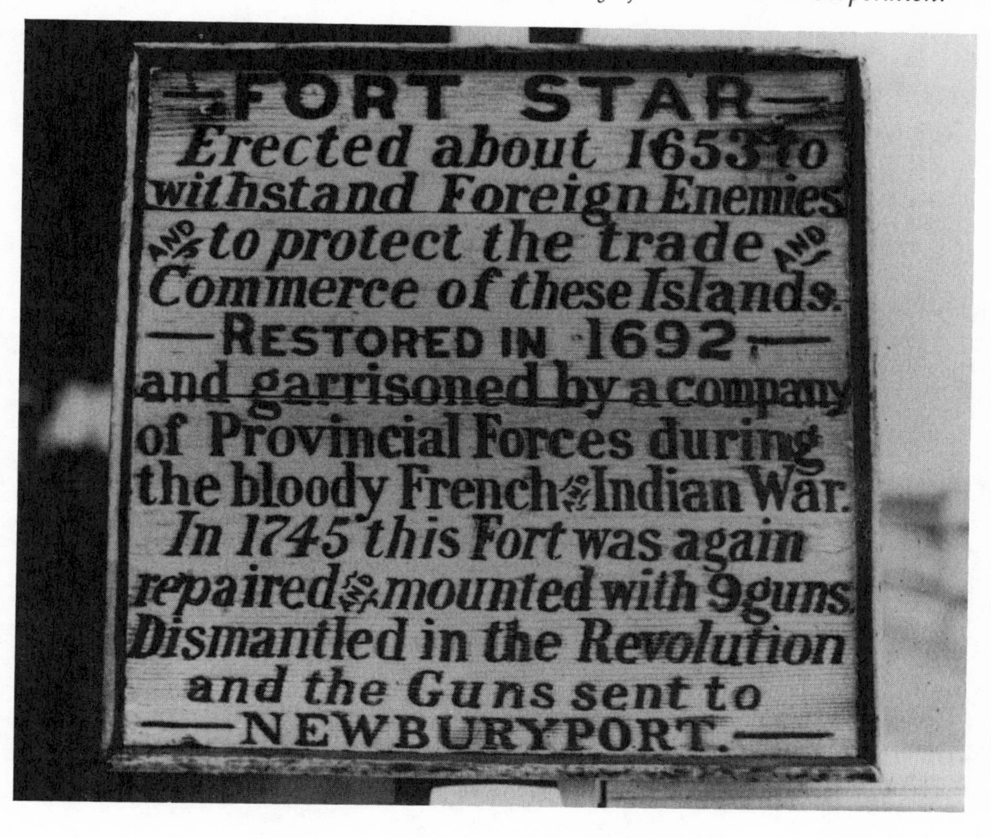

(Above) The old parsonage on Star Island. Note the bird houses on the roof. Courtesy of the Star Island Corporation. (Below) This photograph, taken in 1925, shows the foundation of the Tucke Parsonage. Courtesy of the Portsmouth Public Library.

was ordained in the Gosport meetinghouse in 1732 and served for forty years. The islanders paid his salary in quintals of dunfish, a testament to their respect for him. After Tucke's arrival, there were accurate records of births, deaths, and marriages. Regular meetings were called, officials were elected, and laws passed. Tucke entered the minutes of the meetings into the record book. Typically, laws were passed to control hogs and the mess created by processing fish near the waterfront.

Reverend Tucke was also a physician who served as medical advisor to the members of his church. During his pastorate, the islanders exhibited more thrift and sobriety that they had ever shown before. His salary of a quintal of merchantable dunfish per man was worth approximately 100 pounds, one of the highest salaries paid to a minister in New England at that time. Tucke died in 1773 and was buried on Star Island.

The death of Reverend Tucke marked the end of an era on the islands. Fort Star was dismantled and the nine four-pound cannons were sent to Newburyport. In the early years of the Revolution, the Shoalers were ordered to move to the mainland. The British controlled the sea and John Wentworth, the last royal governor of New Hampshire, had fled to the Islands and later sailed for England. The colonial government could not protect the residents from the British or prevent the British naval vessels from using the islands as a base of operations.

Many families went to Ipswich and Newburyport, Massachusetts, and York, Maine. Several took their houses apart and floated them as rafts to the mainland. The parsonage, built by John Tucke, was reassembled in York Harbor. Some Shoalers wandered back after the war, but the fishing industry never recovered. In 1790, the meetinghouse was burned and there was no attempt to rebuild it. From that time until the close of the century, the islanders were too impoverished to support the ministry. There were no town officers and no regular schools. Marriages were not being performed and cohabitation was common. It was impossible to make a record of ages because no one could remember when children were born. Language had degenerated so badly that it was difficult to understand the people.

Pirates and Buccaneers

It is certain that these islands were a shelter for pirates and freebooters who found traces of their own lawlessness in the lifestyle of the islanders. Here was a convenient place to refit or to acquire fresh provisions without questions being asked. The pirates could expect little booty from the fishermen, but they often used them to replenish their crews.

continued on page 33

Karl Thaxter's photograph of two young women at the turnstile on Appledore. Courtesy of UNH Media Services.

The Courtship Ritual

In her book *Among the Isles of Shoals*, Celia Thaxter described the courtship ritual of the early Shoalers. According to tradition, if a young man became interested in a maid, he hid until she passed by and then he pelted her with small stones. If she turned to check who was throwing the stones, another shower would follow. This was also a sign of interest in the young man. If she went on her way without reacting to the stones, the young man could consider himself rejected.

(Above) This house in York, Maine, was reputed to be one of the houses floated in from the Isles of Shoals during the Revolutionary War period. This photograph was taken in 1952. The building has since been torn down. From the author's collection. (Below) This house in York Harbor is considered to be the original Tucke Parsonage. It was moved from Star Island to the mainland after the Revolutionary War. Photo by John D. Bardwell.

(Above) According to local tradition, this house was moved from the Shoals to York Harbor. It was moved again when the site was purchased for the construction of a summer estate. (Below) The rear section of this building on Sentry Hill in York Harbor was another of the homes that was said to have been floated to York Harbor from the Isles of Shoals. Photos by John D. Bardwell.

The rear section of this York Harbor home on Mercer's Corner is supposed to be a former Shoals house. Photo by John D. Bardwell.

Dixie Bull, the first pirate in New England history, was living in London in 1631. He arrived in Massachusetts Bay in the fall of that year, probably sent to America by Sir Ferdinando Gorges. Bull, a man of adventurous disposition, came from a respectable family and is mentioned with Gorges in a land grant at York, Maine.

After reaching New England, Dixie Bull became a beaver trader. He sailed the coast of Maine, bartering and associating with the Indians. The Pilgrim trading post at Penobscot Bay was one of his favorite stops. This post was raided by a French vessel and Bull was attacked by a French pinnace which captured his shallop, took all his supplies, and left him destitute. Seeking revenge against the French, Bull organized a band of fifteen men and sailed the Maine coast trying to capture a French vessel and recover his losses. Desperate for supplies, Bull confiscated supplies from the pinnaces and shallops of English traders in the area and looted the settlement at Pemaquid. An expedition was organized to search for the pirate, but bad weather delayed the expedition, which was the initial naval demonstration in the colonies. Bull was known to frequent the Isles of Shoals, but the expedition was unable to find him. In 1633, three deserters from Dixie Bull's ship reached home. They suggested that he had gone over to fight for the French. In any event, he never returned to New England.

Philip Babb was one of the earliest and most important residents of the Shoals. He was a constable and tavern keeper who raised cattle, sheep, and hogs in the valley behind his butcher shop on Hog Island. He died in 1671, leaving a substantial estate of 200 pounds. Babb was rumored to have been involved with the pirates, but there is no evidence of that. However, he was supposed to have been so wicked while alive that he was doomed to haunt the island dressed in his striped butcher's frock, with a leather belt around his waist and a sheath for a ghostly butcher's knife which he brandished in the faces of the people he met. In 1852, Nathaniel Hawthorne wrote, "Old Babb, the ghost, has a ring around his neck, and is supposed to have been hung or had his throat cut. There is a luminous appearance about him as he walks, and his face is pale and very dreadful."

Oscar Laighton reported that when he first came to Appledore, there was a large excavation at the head of Babb's Cove, where Philip Babb had dug for treasure. The pit was thirty feet across and ten feet deep. As the story goes, Babb found a chest which was too heavy to remove from the hole. When some friends started to open the cover, smoke, like burning sulphur, came from under the lid. When it was opened, burning horseshoes flew out and the men left the chest in the pit which filled with sand in a storm. For many years, Babb's ghost could be seen at dusk on pleasant evenings, standing at the head of the cove near the pit that he dug. The ghost disappeared after the Coast Guard built a boathouse over the site of his treasure.

Captain John Quelch was a privateer who sailed along the Atlantic coast in a brig under the command of Captain Plowman. They were in search of pirates who had been attacking the shipping along this coast. Plowman died, or was thrown overboard, leaving young Quelch in command of a crew of hardened seamen who convinced him that piracy would be more profitable. His career as a pirate was brief, but in 1950, *Life* magazine reported that in 1702, Captain Quelch was known to have buried $100,000 at the Isles of Shoals, half of which had not been recovered. F. L. Coffman in his book, *1001 Lost, Buried or Sunken Treasures*, claims that Quelch buried treasure in several places on White Island and $275,000 on Star Island.

Quelch was captured after a career of piracy and murder in which he captured nine Portuguese vessels, two fishing boats, a ship, five brigantines and a shallop. The captain and his whole crew were sentenced to die. Six of them, including Quelch, were hanged in Boston in 1704. There is no record of what happened to the other fourteen, or to the treasure that they reportedly buried on the Isles of Shoals.

Edward Teach, alias Blackbeard, was born in Bristol, England, and went to sea at an early age. He served under pirate Benjamin Thornigold who put Teach in charge of a captured French vessel in 1717.

According to legend, Captain Teach often went ashore at the Isles of Shoals where he found shelter on Smuttynose Island. He once returned from England with a woman whom he left on the island to protect a considerable treasure that he buried at that time. Teach sailed away and the woman waited in vain for his return. She died in 1735 and her ghost haunted the island for nearly a century. Many years later, Samuel Haley, while building a wall, turned over a large, flat stone and found four bars of solid silver. Haley used the proceeds to build a breakwater to Malaga. Many believe that he found Blackbeard's treasure.

Others believe that Blackbeard buried his loot on Londoners Island and Haley found treasure buried by Blackbeard's crew. This also included pieces of eight that were buried just below the water line on a beach east of the breakwater at Smuttynose. The pieces of eight have never been found. Mrs. Prudence Randall, owner of Lunging, or Londoners, Island, reported that there were indications of a substantial amount of silver still buried on the landing side of the beach facing Star Island.

According to Charles Chauncy, the cruel pirate Captain Edward Low once captured some fishermen from the Shoals. Low seemed to have developed an overwhelming hatred for New England men and he ordered the captives to be barbarously flogged. He demanded that each of them curse Cotton Mather three times. Mather was in the habit of marching condemned pirates to church on the Sabbath preceding the day on which they were to be executed. There he forced them to listen to a discourse on the torments that awaited them in the other world.

The name of Captain Kidd was once used to threaten disobedient children and the search for his treasure continues to this day. Some believe that he stopped for provisions at the Isles of Shoals and left some of his treasure buried there. However, the record indicates that Kidd was a privateer who was betrayed by his sponsors and did not participate in any acts of piracy. His trial and conviction became a political issue and Captain William Kidd became a scapegoat. His capture of two ships of the Great Mogul that were flying the French flag had antagonized the powerful East India Company and the courts found him guilty of piracy. Kidd was hanged in London on May 23, 1701. His body was preserved in tar and suspended in chains to warn other sailors of the price exacted for piracy on the high seas. In reality, he was probably innocent of piracy.

Captain Scott, who was a comrade of Blackbeard, returned to his homeland after a successful career as a pirate. His boat landed him on a beach near a humble dwelling and he returned carrying a woman. The ship set sail for America and dropped anchor at the Isles of Shoals. He divided the booty with his crew and buried his portion on an island apart

continued on page 38

A true Accompt of all such Gold, Silver, Jewels and Merchandizes, late in the Possession of Capt. William Kid, which have been seized and secured by us under written, Pursuant to an Order from his Excellency Richd. Earle of Bellomont Capt. Generall & Governor in Chief in & over, his Majtys Provinces of ye Massathusets Bay &c bearing date July 9th 1699 Viz.)

	Gold ounces	Silver Ounces	Precious Stones or Jewels
In Capt. William Kid's Boxes			
One Bag qt. 53 Silver Bars		357	
One Bag qt. 79 Bars Silver		442 1/2	
One Bag qt. 74 Bars Silver		421	
One Enameld Silver Box gilt in which are			4 diamonds set in Gold Lockets one diamond loose one large Diamond set in a Gold Ring
Found in Mr. Duncan Campbel's House			
No. 1 - One Bag qt. Gold	58 1/2		
2 - One Bag qt.	94		
3 - One Handkerchiefe qt.	50		
4 - One Bag qt.	103		
5 - One Bag qt.	38 1/2		
6 - One Bag qt.	19 1/4		
7 - One Bag qt.		203	
Also Twenty Dollars, one halfe & one quartr ps of eight, Nine English Crowns, one small Barr of Silver, one small Lump Silver a small Chaine, a small bottle, a Corral Neckace, one ps white & one ps Checkquerd Silk			
In Capt. William Kid's Chest, Two Silver Basons, Two Silver Candlesticks, one Silver Porringer & Som small things of Silver qt.		82	
Rubies small & great Sixty seven, Green stones two One large Loadstone			6 gr

(Above) A list of Captain Kidd's treasure taken at Boston on July 9, 1699, when Kidd was put in jail. From the author's collection. (Opposite) Captain Kidd was hanged in London in 1701. His body was suspended in chains to warn other sailors of the price they could pay for piracy on the high seas. From the author's collection.

from the rest. He lived on the islands with his beautiful companion until a warlike vessel appeared in search of the freebooter. The outlaw took the maiden to the island where he had buried his treasure and made her swear to guard the spot until his return. Both vessels were destroyed in a desperate battle. The pirate's mistress remained true to her oath until she succumbed to want and exposure. Her ghost has been seen more than once on White Island—a tall, shapely figure, wrapped in a long sea cloak, her head and neck uncovered except for a profusion of long, golden hair. Her face is pale and still as marble. She stands on a low projecting point gazing out to sea in an attitude of intense expectation.

Another pirate story involves Dr. Henry Greenland, an ardent Royalist who lived in Kittery, and Richard Cutt, a strict Puritan from Strawbery Banke, now Portsmouth. Apparently Greenland conspired with some pirates to kidnap Cutt and carry him to their ship along with all of his property. He argued that it could be done easily and that they would realize 10,000 pounds for their trouble. The whole affair would be lawful because Cutt had spoken treason against the King. The plot was leaked to Massachusetts authorities and when the pirates left the Isles of Shoals on the *Mermaiden*, she was seized as a pirate vessel and taken to Boston for adjudication.

The founders of the Isles of Shoals did not come on account of their religion, but to fish and trade. They had little sympathy with the religious beliefs of the Plymouth and Massachusetts Bay settlers. What religion they had was Episcopalian and there were no restrictions on gaiety and merriment. The inhabitants supported the Established Church of England, until their annexation to Massachusetts Bay.

The middle of the seventeenth century was the golden age of the Isles of Shoals as a fishing center. Their population was larger than any of the eastern provinces, commerce was extensive, and Gosport harbor was filled with shallops and pinnaces. Their "fearful trade" taught the motley population to be self-reliant and they felt little need for Divine protection and guidance. They exhibited all the reckless and improvident habits of sailors and fishermen—with all their hardihood, courage, and spirit of adventure.

Shipwrecks

The *Nottingham Galley* sailed from London on a trading voyage for Boston on September 25, 1710. The 120-ton vessel carried ten guns and 14 men. It encountered foul weather which prevented the crew from determining its location for ten or twelve days. They sighted the snow-covered coast of New England on December 11th and proceeded on what

The islands have been the scene of many shipwrecks with bodies washed up on the beaches. Courtesy of UNH Media Services.

they concluded was a safe and desirable course, although rain and snow reduced their visibility. At 10 o'clock in the evening *Nottingham Galley* struck the rocks at Boon Island, an uninhabited island within sight of the Isles of Shoals.

The 14-man crew made its way on to the rocky island which had no vegetation or shelter from the cruel storm. Kenneth Roberts, in his book *Boon Island*, describes how the stranded sailors used scraps of canvas to build a shelter. Pieces of cheese and bones of meat which drifted from the wreck supplemented a diet of seaweed and mussels. One man died and was buried "at sea." When a second man died the starving crew decided to "convert the human carcass into the matter of nourishment." The body kept ten of the crew alive until they were rescued by a vessel from Portsmouth on January 4, 1711, after 24 days on the storm-tossed island.

Two crew members made a crude raft and tried to paddle to the mainland for help. One of the bodies and a "raft of ship's tackel" washed up on the beach at Wells. Captain Lewis Bane of York commandeered John Stover's shallop which carried a crew of three. They sailed from Cape Neddick and found the ten men stranded on the tiny island. The sea was so rough that they were unable to rescue the men. In fact, the sea was so rough that the would-be rescuers were unable to return to the harbor. Early the next morning, Stover's shallop was driven up on the shore and destroyed. Bane, Stover, and the others apparently escaped

Captain Fred Miles was operating the two-masted whaleboat when it capsized on July 17, 1902. Fourteen of the seventeen passengers were drowned. Captain Miles survived. Courtesy of William Varrell.

and another vessel was sent out to rescue the men on Boon Island.

On January 14, 1813, the Spanish ship *Sagunto* crashed on the southeast point of Smuttynose in a blinding snowstorm. There are conflicting reports about this shipwreck. According to Celia Thaxter, the great ship of mahogany and cedar crashed on the rocks and the cargo of dried fruits and nuts, bales of broadcloth, and gold and silver was scattered on the shore. Samuel Haley, who lived on the western end of the island, had placed a light in his chamber, but the raging storm drowned out any cries of distress and the Haley family slept quietly through the night. Part of the crew was cast up on the shore and they crawled toward the light. Two of them reached the stone wall in front of the house where they perished. Samuel Haley found them in the morning covered with pure, fresh snow. He gave the alarm and the islanders gathered to provide assistance. Fourteen bodies were found between the wall and the southeast point where the *Sagunto* had broken up. Another body was found during the summer. It was lodged in some bushes near the shore. The victims of the disaster were buried in shallow graves on Smuttynose and a marker was erected to identify the remains of the unknown Spanish sailors.

On July 17, 1902, at 2:20 p.m., the headwaiter at the Oceanic Hotel on Star Island joined his assistant and fourteen waitresses at the dock. Captain Miles loaded the young people into a seventeen-foot whaleboat and took them for an hour-long sail around the islands. As they passed the Appledore wharf on their return to Gosport, the girls rushed to the port rail to get a better view of the steamers and their passengers. Suddenly, the wind shifted and, before Captain Miles could release the sail, the whaleboat rolled over. The heavily ballasted ship sank immediately, pulling many people under. The girls, with air trapped under their long skirts, first bobbed to the surface, but they were pulled under when their skirts became water-soaked. The captain, who couldn't swim, came to the surface beside a wooden soapbox. Two waiters who were strong swimmers died trying to save the others. Two of the waitresses were pulled from the water and Captain Miles floated ashore on the wooden box. They were the only survivors. Three sets of sisters died in the tragedy, probably the worst to occur in the area.

Seacoast residents were shocked on May 23, 1939, when they learned that the submarine USS *Squalus* had sunk in 240 feet of water while on sea trials off the Isles of Shoals. A sister ship, the USS *Sculpin*, had located the *Squalus* and rescue vessels were rushed to the scene. The McCann rescue chamber was brought from New London and the first of 33 survivors was brought up on May 24. Twenty-six officers and men were lost. After several unsuccessful attempts, the submarine was raised on September 13. The *Squalus* was towed to the Portsmouth Naval Shipyard. Rebuilt and recommissioned as the USS *Sailfish*, this submarine distinguished herself with an excellent war record in World War II.

The British freighter *Empire Knight* crashed into Boon Island Ledge during a raging blizzard on February 11, 1944. Navy and Coast Guard ships stood by in the howling snowstorm, but they were unable to get close enough to take off the 44 members of her crew.

The freighter carrying "general cargo" (military secrecy prevented reporters from being more specific) was swept onto the rocks and pounded by mountainous waves throughout the night. Most of the lifesaving equipment was swept away when the ship hit the reef so the captain decided to remain aboard and try to save her. The *Empire Knight*

continued on page 47

(Above) The Pinafore *tied up at the dock at Appledore. Courtesy of UNH Media Services. (Right) The* Samuel Gaucher *was wrecked on Duck Island Reef on November 11, 1911. It was loaded with coal en route from Newport to Portland when it went aground in the fog. Courtesy of UNH Media Services.*

Reports of Shipwrecks on the Isles of Shoals

The first news from the Shoals since the storm was brought in on Tuesday by one of Newton's fishermen. The gale was terrific. The little steamer *Pinafore* was sunk at her mooring and an entire section of the piazza about the Oceanic carried away. The loss to the hotels, buildings and cottages will probably amount to $4,000.

Portsmouth Daily Chronicle
Wednesday, November 30, 1898

The schooner *Samuel J. Gaucher* was wrecked on November 11, 1911, approximately 500 yards from Duck Island with a load of 4,000 tons of coal. Her crew of thirteen men were taken off by the Isles of Shoals life saving crew. The big five-masted schooner was a total loss. Bound from Newport to Portland, she was anchored under the lee of White Island in a dense fog. In the morning, the vessel started to get under way and went on to Duck Island Reef at high tide making a large hole in her bottom. They were spotted by Captain Staples and the crew of the Appledore life saving station took off Captain McGrath and his crew of twelve men.

Portsmouth Daily Chronicle
Portsmouth Herald
Saturday, November 11, 1911

It was this year (1858) that the *Springbird* was lost in a fierce gale from the northwest. She was fast to her mooring off Appledore when the chain parted and she came ashore near the landing, a total wreck in the heavy sea. We were troubled about getting another vessel for our line to Portsmouth, but finally arranged with Henry and Charles Becker to run their schooner which was a good-sized, able boat.

Ninety Years at the Isles of Shoals
Oscar Laighton

(Above) Launching of the USS Squalus *at Portsmouth Naval Shipyard on September 14, 1938. (Below) Men from the USS* Falcon *struggle to bring the sunken sub to the surface on May 23, 1939. U.S. Navy photos.*

(Above) USS Squalus *in berth. The battered conning tower was damaged by bumping against a pontoon while it was being lifted. (Below) USS* Squalus, SS192, *at berth during pumping-out operations in September, 1939. U.S. Navy photos.*

The McCann rescue chamber was used to remove officers and crew from the sunken submarine. The first of the 33 survivors were brought up on May 24, 1939. U.S. Navy photo.

began to break up during the night and word was given to abandon ship. A short time later, the ship broke in two. The forward part remained on the rocks and the aft was carried away to sink in deep water.

Chief Engineer Sven Haagensen was one of nineteen men who leaped into the 50-foot waves when the ship broke in two. He managed to get into a lifeboat with the second mate. Other survivors clung to rafts and large planks. Chief Wireless Officer Stanley J. Wood was credited with saving at least seven lives by pulling men from the water into his boat. Navy and Coast Guard boats picked up three survivors and thirteen bodies were recovered later. Twenty-four members of the crew were lost in the disaster.

White Island light from a painting by W. F. DeHass.

Life in the Grand Hotels

IN 1831, THOMAS LAIGHTON WAS EMPLOYED as a clerk in the U. S. Customs House in Portsmouth. Laighton was anxious to establish himself in business and was fascinated by an upcoming auction of three islands formerly owned by Benjamin Haley at the Isles of Shoals. Hog, Smuttynose, and Malaga comprised the largest part of the group. A dream of re-establishing the fishing industry on the islands attracted him to the auction, but Laighton watched with dismay while John Smiley became the successful bidder. However, Thomas Laighton continued to pursue his dream and, in 1839, he and Joseph Cheever jointly purchased the three islands and Cedar Island as well.

It was at that time that the post of lighthouse keeper on White Island became available. Thomas applied for the post where he could oversee his own islands and support the fishing industry. Eliza, who had never ventured beyond the mouth of Portsmouth harbor, moved to the lighthouse and made her home in the small, sturdy, white-washed cottage provided for the keeper and his family. Their daughter, Celia Laighton, was four years old at the time and Oscar was only a baby. They moved from a secure little house on a quiet street in rural New England to a barren island that was frequently inaccessible because of the dangerous landing. Six nautical miles of ocean lay between them and the mainland. During the first winter a storm washed away the boats and destroyed the covered walk that led to the light. Hens and henhouses were carried out to sea. The only way that they could save the cow was to bring her into the kitchen.

The lighthouse keeper was supplied with an eighteen-foot sailboat and a dory which Thomas Laighton used to visit Smuttynose or Hog Island to check on the fishermen whom he had employed to catch fish for

continued on page 55

(Right) A broadside announcing the sale of land on Smuttynose in 1831. Courtesy of the Star Island Corporation. (Far Right) A map of the Town of Gosport on Star Island redrawn from a detail of the Rockingham County map of 1857. Courtesy of the Rye Historical Society.

AUCTION.

To be sold at Public Auction at J. L. Lawrence, Esqr's dwelling-house, at Kittery Point, in the County of York,

On WEDNESDAY the
12th of October next, at 11 o'clock A. M.

By virtue of a license from the Hon. Wm. A. Hayes, Esq. Judge of Probate within and for the County of York and State of Maine,

All the right, title, interest, and demands that Benjamin Haley, late of Portsmouth, in the County of Rockingham, State of New-Hampshire, mariner, deceased, had, at the time of his decease, in and unto the island, commonly called Hog Island, one of the Isle of Shoals, in said County of York.

Also, all the right, title, and demands that said Haley had at the time of his decease, in and unto the islands commonly called Smutty Nose and Malaga Islands; together with all the said Haley's right he had at the time of his decease, to a large two story DWELLING HOUSE, lately built by said Haley, and his right to a number of other Buildings, all of which are on said Smutty Nose Island, with the Dock and Water Privilege; to be sold to raise twenty-two hundred and twenty-five dollars to pay the claims and demands against the said Haley's estate, with incidental charges.

Conditions of sale will be made known at the time and place of sale.

ELIZA H. HALEY,
Administratrix.

Sept. 6, 1831.

TOWN OF GOSPORT
1 8 5 7

D Haley's Inlet
Great Cove
Little Cove
Jacobs Inlet
Ram's Horn Cove
Salter's Point
Bragg's Cove
R. G. Haley &
R. L. Randall
D. Haley & S.H. Robinson
Cem.
J. Caswell
J. Caswell
W.C. Newton
G. Randall
J. W.&I.G. Randall
J. B. Downs
W. Downs
W. Robinson
N.F. Berry
W. Caswell
J. M. Caswell
School House
Church
Rev. G. Beebe
Cem.
Sandy Cove
L. B. Caswell's Hotel
Trackle Cove
Capt Downs Point
Steven's Pt
Schelly Cove
Sampson's Spring
U.S. Coast Survey Station
Heater
Southern Point
STAR ISLAND
Lump Pond
Betty Moody's Hole
High Bluff
Long Canoe
Middle Point

Redrawn from a detail of the Rockingham County Map of 1857. Issued by the Rye Historical Society 1973

(Above) The buildings on White Island in 1860. Courtesy of the National Archives.
(Below) White Island lighthouse as it looked in 1977. Photo by Gary Samson.

(Above) The winding stairs in the lighthouse tower. (Right) The lamps in the White Island lighthouse were kept cleaned and polished by the Coast Guard personnel who were assigned to service the light. Photos by Gary Samson.

(Above) A photograph of White Island and Seavey's Island taken from the lighthouse. The two islands are separated at high tide but are joined when the tide is low. Photo by Gary Samson. (Below) An earlier view of the White Island lighthouse station. Courtesy of William Varrell.

(Above) The Mid-Ocean House of Entertainment was Thomas Laighton's first experience in the tourist business. (Below) A cow rests in front of the Haley house on Smuttynose while a guest tries to catch up on her correspondence. Courtesy of the Portsmouth Public Library.

Trap dikes and other geologic features of the islands have stimulated the creative energies of artists and photographers. (Below) Fishermen have worked the waters of the Isles of Shoals for more than three centuries. Peter E. Randall photographs.

Sunset from Appledore. Peter E. Randall photograph.

Two views of Celia Thaxter's garden on Appledore which has been recreated by the Shoals Marine Laboratory on the exact site of the poet's original nineteenth century garden. The photograph below shows the laboratory buildings on the hill behind the garden. Peter E. Randall photographs.

Colorful foul weather gear is always ready for use by the students and faculty of the Shoals Marine Laboratory. Courtesy of UNH Media Services. (Below) The lush marine life of the intertidal zone is the prime study area for students of Shoals Marine Laboratory. Peter E. Randall photograph.

Crashing waves emphasize the need for a lighthouse on White Island. Home to lighthouse keepers for 150 years, the facility is now automated. (Below) The century-old Oceanic Hotel and the Caswell Cemetery recall the Victorian years when summer vacationers sojourned on Star Island. Peter E. Randall photographs.

Among the varied nesting seabirds on the Isles of Shoals are double-crested cormorants, here photographed on Duck Island. (Below) Snowy egrets nest on Appledore Island in a colony which includes glossy ibis, black-crowned night heron, and little blue heron. Peter E. Randall photographs.

An aerial view of the Isles of Shoals. Clockwise from top left are the islands of Appledore, Smuttynose and Malaga, Cedar, Star, White and Seavey's and Lunging. (Below) The great black-backed gull colony on Smuttynose is one of the largest in the world, numbering some 1,300 nesting pairs. Peter E. Randall photographs.

Candlelight services are held nightly in the Gosport Church during the conference season on Star Island. (Below) The Gosport Church is one of the oldest buildings on Star Island, constructed in 1800. The other stone structures, including the Vaughn Cottege at left, and the Parker Memorial at right, have been built since 1948. Peter E. Randall photographs.

him to sell. When Laighton unexpectedly was elected to the New Hampshire Legislature, a substitute light keeper came to White Island. The Laightons moved to Samuel Haley's house on nearby Smuttynose Island which was built with timbers from the wreck of the Spanish ship in which fifteen sailors had lost their lives. The large, roomy house had been named "The Mid-Ocean House of Entertainment." Eliza Laighton dusted off the sign and ran an inn during the summer months. Among the early visitors were Richard Henry Dana, a young author, John Weiss, a theological student, and Levi Lincoln Thaxter, a recent graduate of Harvard College. The Laightons returned to White Island when Thomas ended his two-year term in the legislature, but he had now decided that a modern hotel on Hog Island would be more promising than the old inn or the fishing business.

In 1847, Thomas Laighton sold his share of some family holdings at the north end of Portsmouth to the railroad interests. This provided some of the capital needed to build a hotel on the Isles of Shoals. Levi Thaxter's enthusiasm for the project helped convince his father, a wealthy banker, to advance a loan for the project. Hog Island was renamed Appledore. Thomas Laighton and Levi Thaxter entered into an agreement to build the Appledore Hotel and the building materials were ordered from Bangor, Maine. They were delivered to Appledore on one of the sailing ships owned by Laighton's brothers, workmen were brought over from the mainland, and the era of tourism was about to begin.

Celia was twelve years old when her father resigned his position as lighthouse keeper and moved his family to Appledore. A Mr. Baker took over the lighthouse and John Randall moved to Smuttynose to manage the fishing business. Thomas Laighton was busy with the construction of the hotel so Levi Thaxter became the tutor for the three children. The work went on throughout the winter and the Appledore House opened for business on June 15, 1848. The trickle of guests increased as word of the new hotel reached people on the mainland. The Laighton boys started their own lobster business and the fame of Eliza's chowder brought many curious visitors.

Levi Thaxter soon lost interest in the business and agreed to dissolve his partnership in the hotel business with Thomas Laighton. However, his growing interest in Celia convinced Thomas to send her to the Mount Washington Female Seminary in South Boston. The relationship between Levi and Celia became more intense and Levi asked for her hand in marriage. Her father felt that she was too young to be married but did agree to an engagement. On September 30, 1851, after the hotel guests were gone, 16-year-old Celia Laighton and 30-year-old Levi Thaxter were married in the parlor of the Appledore House. After the

continued on page 61

(Above) The lobby of the Appledore Hotel with flowers on the counter and the wings of an owl over the fireplace. (Below) A sketch of the original Appledore hotel from a lantern slide. Courtesy UNH Media Services.

APPLEDORE HOUSE,

ISLES OF SHOALS.

LAIGHTON BROTHERS & CO. - - - PROPRIETORS.

(Above) From the Appledore House letterhead in 1878. Courtesy of the Portsmouth Public Library. (Below) The Haley house with three guests on the porch. Photo by G. W. Patch of Portsmouth. Courtesy of UNH Media Services.

(Above) In 1902, this horse was used to haul luggage from the steamboat landing to the hotel. From Oscar Laighton's scrapbook. Courtesy of the Star Island Corporation. (Right) The dining room of the Appledore House is set for dinner. Courtesy of the Portsmouth Public Library.

(Above) The Mount Washington Female Seminary in South Boston, Massachusetts. Courtesy of the Portsmouth Public Library. (Below) Celia Laighton at 15 years of age. Courtesy of UNH Media Services.

Nathaniel Hawthorne came to the islands with Franklin Pierce, and his comments are recorded in his American Notebooks. *Courtesy of UNH Media Services.*

Nathaniel Hawthorne and Franklin Pierce

Nathaniel Hawthorne came to Appledore in 1852 to meet his old Bowdoin classmate Franklin Pierce who had been nominated by the Democratic National Convention to be their candidate for President of the United States. Hawthorne had published *The Scarlet Letter* in 1850 and had just completed *The House of Seven Gables*. Pierce wanted his former classmate to write his campaign biography, an assignment that was totally out of character for Hawthorne. He accepted out of personal loyalty to a friend but would never list the biography among his writings.

Hawthorne arrived on August 30th and spent most of his time exploring the islands. He visited with the natives and copied the *Gosport Church Records*, which he found in the possession of the town clerk. After a visit with Celia and Levi in the North Cottage the writer commented, "This is certainly a romantic incident to find such a young man on this lonely island; his marriage to this pretty Miranda is a true romance....What he will do on returning to the world (as his purpose is) I cannot imagine; but, no doubt, through all their remaining life, both he and she will look back to this rocky ledge, with its handful of soil, as to a Paradise."

(Left) Bret Harte was one of the writers who was attracted to the islands. Courtesy of the Star Island Corporation. (Right) Professor Louis Agassiz was another of the well-known visitors on the Isles of Shoals. Courtesy of Rosamond Thaxter.

wedding, the young couple left to visit Levi's family in Watertown, Massachusetts. Celia Thaxter left the isolation of her rocky island home and moved to an urban community that offered many opportunities for her to encounter music, art, and literature.

Appledore began to attract many famous visitors who returned each summer. Franklin Pierce, who later became President, brought his wife and son. Levi Thaxter and John Weiss were attracting many of New England's outstanding writers and artists to the island. John Greenleaf Whittier and his sister Elizabeth, James T. Fields, Thomas Bailey Aldrich, James Russell Lowell, and William Morris Hunt were among the first to summer there. Nathaniel Hawthorne came with a letter of introduction from Franklin Pierce. He was greatly interested in the islands and had Oscar Laighton sail him to White and Star islands.

Celia's first child, Karl, was the first baby born on Appledore in many years. He was delivered by a mid-wife summoned from Gosport on Star Island and he may have suffered birth injuries that left him with a slight limp. John was born two years later in Newburyport, Massachusetts, and Roland was born four years later in Newtonville. The Thaxters now had been married for eight years and they had three young sons. However, a number of forces were working to divide them and impact upon their life together.

Levi had to devote a great deal of time to his aged parents in Watertown while Celia's family was anxious for her to join them on the Isles of Shoals, particularly during the summers. In the fall of 1855, Levi and Oscar were caught in a storm while sailing back to the islands from

(Above) Celia Thaxter's home at 542 California Street, Newtonville, Massachusetts. Courtesy of the Portsmouth Public Library. (Below) Horsepower was used to pull the boats from the water at the end of each season. This boat is being pulled through the Appledore tennis court in front of Celia Thaxter's cottage. Courtesy of UNH Media Services.

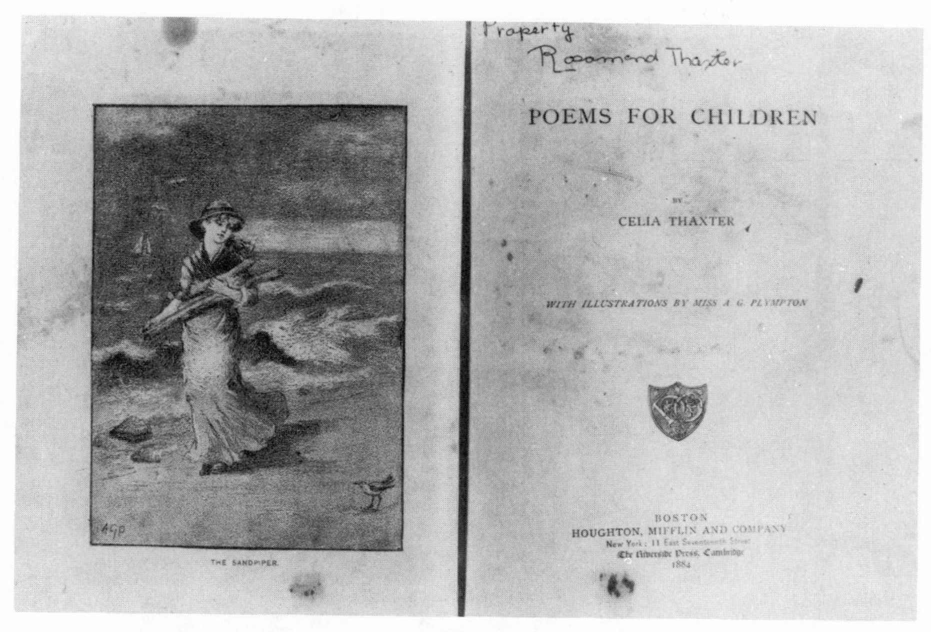

An 1884 edition of Celia Thaxter's Poems for Children *which included her oft-quoted poem,* The Sandpiper. *Courtesy of the Portsmouth Public Library.*

Portsmouth. They were shipwrecked on the rocks of Appledore and were lucky to escape with their lives. Levi was so shaken by the experience that he determined never to return to the islands. From that time, Celia traveled to Appledore without her husband.

The publication of Celia Thaxter's first poem, "Land-locked," in the *Atlantic Monthly* was more than a reflection of her loneliness for her family and their island home. Writing poetry became a new outlet for the young woman and she was given every opportunity to meet the most celebrated literary figures of the day. She wrote "Expectation," "The Sandpiper," and "Spanish Graves." In the spring of 1869, she began a series of articles that eventually was published as *Among the Isles of Shoals*. Soon, every poem that Celia offered for publication was gladly accepted.

In the meantime, Levi was unable to settle upon an occupation that suited him. He became interested in ornithology and began taking long trips to collect specimens. His wife took advantage of his absence to spend summers at Appledore with her sons. When Karl's handicaps prevented him from attending school, he remained with his mother while John and Roland traveled with their father. Celia's parents were in poor health and she continued to spend long summers on Appledore.

Another factor that contributed to the separation of Celia and

continued on page 71

The dock at Smuttynose with Star Island in the background. Courtesy of UNH Media Services.

Organized Prize Fighting

Organized prize fighting was illegal in the 1860s and it was difficult to conduct fights in urban areas that had well organized police forces. Promoters looked for isolated locations with easy accessibility and little concern for law enforcement. This described conditions at the Isles of Shoals since the days when it was a port-of-call for pirates and privateers.

Apparently, a fair number of prizefights took place at the Shoals and others were cancelled to avoid clashes with the law. One such fight took place on October 2, 1867, between Mathew "Rocky" Moore of New York City and George Rooke from Providence. Both fighters weighed in at 145 pounds. The fight took place on a 24-foot-square plot of grass near Christian Johnson's house on Smuttynose. Spectators arrived on steamers, schooners, and a fleet of small sailboats.

The fight lasted for one hour and twenty-five minutes. Each round lasted until there was a knockdown and the fight ended in the 25th round when Rooke's seconds threw in the sponge and Moore was declared the winner. It was a winner-take-all match but Moore gave Rooke $50 for his participation.

A second event was planned to promote three fights. The first was between an Englishman who weighed 112 lbs and an Irishman who weighed 114. The second event featured George Cheer fighting Baker from Bangor, and the third bout was between two men from Boston. Stormy weather prevented the steamboats from bringing the spectators but several sailboats left, one bringing the contestants for the main event. After long delays and a rough trip the ships reached the island. That was the good news. The bad news was that the steamboat carrying the purse money had not arrived and two fighters were too seasick to do any fighting. The return trip only added to their discomfort and the fighters were convinced that they should not participate in future fights if they were held on an island.

Cedric Laighton, who was upset that such disgraceful and beastly exhibitions should be held at the islands, reported that the fog had one good effect for it so disgusted the prizefighters that they must have given up. "They were most horribly seasick, both coming out and going in, and the steamer from Boston got lost in the fog and had to put back."

Levi Thaxter and his son Roland dressed for a hunting trip in 1868. Courtesy of UNH Media Services.

(Above) Another view of Celia's parlor decorated with flowers from her garden and artwork supplied by her friends. Courtesy of UNH Media Services. (Left) The mantle decorated with flowers in the parlor of Celia Thaxter's cottage. Courtesy of the Portsmouth Public Library.

(Left) Relaxing on the porch was a favorite island pastime and reading was an approved activity for ladies in 1900. (Below) Colonel Fuller on the hotel porch "engaging in his favorite pastime." Courtesy of John Hutchinson.

Celia Thaxter's famous parlor decorated with the works of her favorite artists and the flowers from her equally famous garden. Courtesy of UNH Media Services.

(Above) A group of young pirates searching for victims in the Appledore pool.
(Below) The men are pulling the boats up for storage at the end of the summer season.
Courtesy of John Hutchinson.

Known successively as the red house, the Johnson house and the Hontvet house, this building was the site of the Smuttynose murders. Courtesy of the Portsmouth Public Library.

Levi was that her presence on Appledore attracted many guests to the hotel. Artists, writers, and musicians were regular visitors to her cottage which became an art gallery and social center. She wrote, read, and discussed her work with her friends. She cultivated her legendary garden which produced the flowers that decorated the cottage. Celia began to feel indispensable at the Shoals, and in the mid-1870s she spent four consecutive winters on Appledore while Levi lived in the shabby house in Newtonville. Celia's books, *Poems* and *Among the Isles of Shoals*, had been well received and she began to experience financial independence from a husband who had never been a good provider. In 1875, she wrote *A Memorable Murder*, to do her best to insure that the murderer of two Norwegian women on Smuttynose Island would receive just punishment for his fiendish crime.

As the story goes, John and Maren Hontvet, Ivan and Anethe Christensen, Ivan's sister Karen and John's brother Matthew wintered on Smuttynose. Karen had been Eliza Laighton's companion until late February, 1873, when she was dismissed for fussing over a request to "wash and sweep out the workmen's quarters." She left Appledore and returned to live with her relatives on Smuttynose. On the night of March

Dorothy Ahlgren and Gary Samson filming The Ballad of Louis Wagner, *which describes the terrible murders on Smuttynose. Photo by Karen Swanson. Courtesy of UHN Media Services.*

5th, the men were in Portsmouth to sell their catch and buy bait. Louis Wagner, a drifter who had been befriended by the young Norwegians, rowed to the island and killed Karen and Anethe with an ax. Maren escaped through a window, barefooted and in her nightgown. She fled with her little dog over the icy rocks and hid by a large rock on the far side of the island. Unable to find her, Wagner ransacked the house, but found only $15. He apparently rowed back to the mainland and arrived in Rye just as the sun was rising.

As soon as the sun came up, Maren crawled to Malaga Island where she attracted the attention of the Ingebertsen family on Appledore. Jorge, the father of the family, took her to his home and sent for the Laightons. She was bruised and bloodstained and her feet were frozen. Meanwhile, Wagner bought a new suit of clothes and caught the train for Boston. When news of the crime reached the mainland, he was quickly apprehended and returned to Portsmouth. An angry mob tried to lynch him when he was moved from the railroad station to the jail. Later, he was turned over to Maine authorities, because Smuttynose was under the jurisdiction of the state of Maine.

Wagner was tried, convicted, and sentenced to death. He continued to proclaim his innocence and many people were convinced that he

continued on page 79

Louis Wagner and the Christensen brothers in Portsmouth on the day before the murders. From the film The Ballad of Louis Wagner. *Photo by Karen Swanson. Courtesy of UNH Media Services.*

(Above) Louis Wagner, left, in the custody of Sheriff A. J. Scruton of Farmington. (Right) The ax used to murder the two women was found by the coroner near the front door of the Hontvet house. Photos by Gary Samson. Courtesy of Mrs. Earl S. Flanders.

Fires in Gosport

Following the Civil War, there were a series of fires in Gosport that destroyed nine buildings. The barn on Smuttynose burned from unknown causes late in April, 1866. A week later, the barn at the Atlantic House was found burning in the night. The rapidly spreading flames consumed the Atlantic House, the Gosport House, the home of Mrs. Nathaniel Berry, and six barns and sheds. Fire has always been a threat to the islanders because there was no fire fighting equipment and strong winds caused flames to spread quickly through the dry wooden structures.

The burning of Gosport's two hotels created a need for accommodations on the island. Elvin Newton opened his home and called it the Newton House. However, it wasn't large enough to accept the overflow of the Appledore House which was attracting more guests that it could handle. Lemuel Caswell rebuilt the Atlantic House which opened in 1869. Origen Caswell replaced the Gosport House in 1871. The two hotels were really no more than large houses but the linen was fresh and Gosport wasn't a center of fashion.

John Poor bought out many Gosport residents and built the magnificent Oceanic Hotel in 1873. Apparently, one of the stipulations of the sale was that he pay the town's war debts. The luxurious Victorian hotel had a boat landing, an elevator, broad piazzas, and modern appointments. Visitors were attracted by the news of the murders on Smuttynose and a yacht race between Star and Boon Island which attracted the finest yachts on the East coast. After three successful seasons, there were plans to build a large addition, add a swimming pool, and restore Fort Star as a tourist attraction. On November 11, 1875, while the workmen were building the addition, the Oceanic burned to the ground. In order to provide a replacement for the upcoming summer season, the lumber for the addition was used to join the Gosport and Atlantic houses which became the second Oceanic hotel. This hotel still operates as the Star Island Conference Center.

(Above) The Gosport House rebuilt in 1871. (Below) The Gosport House and the Atlantic House as they appeared on August 24, 1871. Both original hotels had been destroyed by fire in 1866. From a stereoview by the Davis Brothers of Portsmouth, N.H. Courtesy of the Portsmouth Public Library.

(Above) Gosport Village on Star Island in 1873–1875. The first Oceanic Hotel built by John Poor is on the far left. The second Gosport House, center, and the second Atlantic House, far right, were repositioned and joined by an addition to become the current Oceanic Hotel seen below. From a stereoview by the Davis Brothers of Portsmouth, N.H. Courtesy of the Portsmouth Public Library. (Below) The Gosport House and the Atlantic House were combined into one complex to form the second Oceanic Hotel after the first one burned in 1875. Courtesy of UNH Media Services.

(Above) The Laighton house on Appledore was constructed in 1881. Courtesy of the Star Island Corporation. (Below) The porch of the first Oceanic Hotel on Star Island. From a stereograph by the Davis Brothers. Courtesy of William Varrell.

could not row to the Shoals and back in one night. Ironically, Louis Wagner was one of the last men to be hanged in the state of Maine. Shortly after his death, capital punishment was abolished.

Oscar and Cedric took over the management of the Appledore House after their father died in 1866. They bought Celia's share of Appledore and built an addition on the hotel. In 1871, John Poor visited Appledore and Star. On Appledore he found a flourishing resort. On Star he found the small Gosport House in need of repair and a few fishermen in their shabby homes. Poor bought most of the property on the island, including the Meetinghouse and Gosport House in 1872, and all the residents moved to Portsmouth. In 1873, Poor spent $35,000 to build the Oceanic Hotel and the Laightons had competition for the first time. The following year they reluctantly agreed to build a landing pier at Appledore and acquired a small fleet of pleasure boats for the guests. On November 11, 1875, the Oceanic burned to the ground. Poor decided to rebuild by incorporating the Gosport House and the Atlantic House in the new hotel. However, the project went badly, the weather was unpleasant and many reservations were cancelled. He became discouraged and offered to sell the property to the Laighton brothers for $100,000. Mrs. Laighton and Cedric were opposed to increasing their debts, but they worried about who might buy the hotel if they didn't. They purchased it in 1877 and Cedric became responsible for its operation. Operating the two establishments on islands in the ocean was a logistical challenge, but they flourished for another twenty-five years. Mrs. Laighton died a year after they purchased the Oceanic, but Celia came to handle all the correspondence about reservations. She often lingered in the fall when the guests were gone and the islands were bathed in Indian summer. It was difficult for her to become a wife and mother in Newtonville after being the center of attention on the island during the summer. She was very close to her brothers, Oscar and Cedric, with whom she spent most of eight winters on the lonely and isolated islands. Her son Karl, with his physical and mental disabilities, was a constant burden and she welcomed the support of her family.

It was during the long winters that Celia Thaxter began painting on china. Her first attempts were quite successful and she began painting little pitchers and vases with images drawn from nature. She illustrated her books of poems and painted on tiles, plates, cups, and saucers. This new skill added to her income and her financial independence. William Morris Hunt, Appleton Brown, and other artist friends helped to develop her talent.

Levi agreed to return to Appledore during the summer of 1879, and Celia had all members of her family together for the first time in

continued on page 89

(Above) The first Oceanic Hotel on Star Island was built by John Poor in 1873 and it burned in 1875. From a stereograph by the Davis Brothers. Courtesy of the Portsmouth Public Library. (Below) Two of the senior residents are going for a row around the cove. c. 1900. Courtesy of John Hutchinson.

(Above) An aerial view of Star Island in 1950. Photo by Paul Marston of Portsmouth, N.H. Courtesy of the Portsmouth Public Library. (Below) A Star Island visitor is warmly dressed and carrying her umbrella. The windmill can be seen on the right. Courtesy of the Star Island Corporation.

(Above) The old barn on Star Island where the livestock were kept. (Below) Turkeys were raised on the islands to supply the tables in the hotel dining rooms. c. 1912. Courtesy of the Star Island Corporation.

(Above) A small amount of hay was cut on the islands to feed livestock which included horses, cows and sheep. Courtesy of the Portsmouth Public Library. (Below) The south gate on Appledore. The gate could be closed to prevent livestock from wandering into the area occupied by the guests. Courtesy of John Hutchinson.

(Above) One of the major projects was laying a cable between Star and Appledore to improve communication between the two islands. Courtesy of John Hutchinson. (Below) Cutting ice on the small pond on Star Island. Ice was stored to supply the hotels in the summer. Courtesy of the Portsmouth Public Library.

(Above) Workmen cutting ice to be stored in the ice house for later use. Courtesy of the Portsmouth Public Library. (Below) The ice house and ice pond on Appledore as they appeared in 1922. Star Island can be seen in the background. Courtesy of the Star Island Corporation.

Celia Thaxter at her painting table. From a lantern slide. Courtesy of the Portsmouth Public Library.

(Above) William Morris Hunt, an artist, was a close friend of Celia's and a regular summer visitor. Courtesy of the Star Island Corporation. (Right) Mrs. William Morris Hunt. Courtesy of the Star Island Corporation.

The Death of William Morris Hunt

William Morris Hunt was ill in mind and body during the summer of 1879. The celebrated artist was watched carefully to be sure that he didn't hurt himself on the rocky island. On a stormy afternoon he left the cottage where Celia was painting, and disappeared into the storm. Two hours passed and he did not return. Searchers looked for him and it was Celia's fate to find him face down in a small pond on the north side of the island. They carried Hunt back to the cottage and tried to revive him, but he had been dead for hours.

The tragedy disrupted an otherwise happy summer which saw Levi returning to Appledore for the first time in many years. A memorial exhibition of Hunt's work was prepared for showing at the Boston Art Museum in the fall and it was well attended.

(Above) Celia's cottage. The poet is standing on the edge of the porch and five or six other people are peeking at the camera man from various hiding places. Courtesy of UNH Media Services. (Below) The Appledore Hotel lobby and desk decorated with artwork and flowers. Courtesy of the Star Island Corporation.

many years. He was attracted by his friend William Morris Hunt, who was ill and mentally unstable. The happy reunion ended abruptly when Hunt went out in a storm and was found dead, face down in a little pond on the island.

The 1880s were Celia's happiest years on Appledore. She would arrive in March with baskets of seedlings to transplant in her garden. She stayed with her brother Oscar until the weather was warm enough to move into her unheated cottage. She helped supervize the work of the Norwegian girls from Smuttynose who were hired to help open the hotel. Carpenters and other workmen were usually working on new cottages or repairing old ones.

The Appledore House had evolved into three sections connected by a long piazza lined with rocking chairs. From here guests could see the boardwalk and dock where the steamers arrived twice daily with passengers, supplies, and mail. A small fleet of pleasure boats was anchored in Gosport Harbor when they weren't sailing around the islands. Swimmers in their elaborate attire enjoyed the swimming pool that had been created in Babb's Cove. During the peak years, over 500 people lived on the island. This included hotel guests, an army of employees, and people who owned cottages on the island.

Celia's greatly enlarged parlor became the gathering place for the artistic and talented people who considered it a privilege to visit there. The room was filled with comfortable sofas and easy chairs, upholstered in olive green. Her friends could listen to music, conversation, stories, or poetry reading. Every inch of wall space was covered with sketches in water color, oil, and pastel. Here was displayed the work of J. Appleton Brown, Ellen Robbins, Childe Hassam and many others. There were photographs of famous places that had been sent by friends. Easels held the work of artists that were offered for sale.

Over the years, Celia's circle included Lowell, Longfellow, Whittier, the Fieldses, Sarah Jewett, William Dean Howells, and Thomas Bailey Aldrich. Beethoven sonatas were played on the piano, or Eichberg, Ole Bull, and Van Ronte played their violins. Occasionally someone would sing. Everywhere there were Celia's beautiful and unusual flower arrangements. They adorned the tables, mantels, and windowsills. Sweet peas, poppies, red roses, and nasturtiums were displayed in bowls, baskets, and tall cylinders.

Celia's garden became an island landmark and many visitors urged her to share her secrets in print. At the end of the season of 1893, she returned to Portsmouth with her notes and began work on the book. *An Island Garden* was published in the spring of 1894. Illustrated with colorful paintings by Childe Hassam, the book was very well received

continued on page 113

(Above) The Appledore House and cottages. Only the two buildings at right are still standing. Courtesy of UNH Media Services. (Below) Guests relaxing on the porch of the Appledore House. Courtesy of the Star Island Corporation.

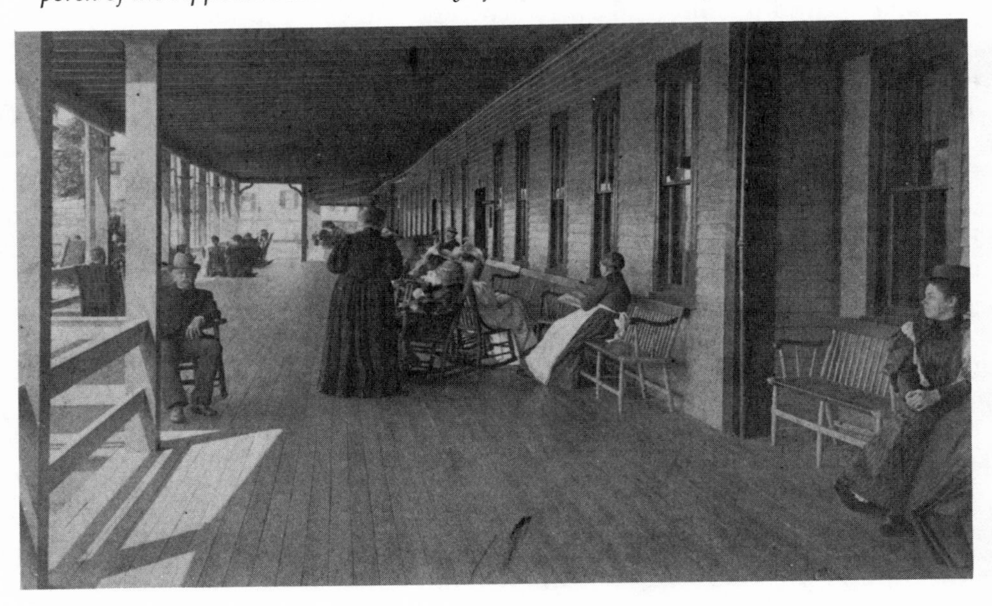

(Above) Tub races in the pool were a popular form of entertainment in 1899. (Below) The men's bathhouses at the edge of the Appledore pool. The ladies' bathhouses were appropriately located on the other side of the pool. Courtesy of John Hutchinson.

(Above) Many young Shoalers got their first sailing lessons in the pool near the Appledore Hotel. (Below) Rafting in the pool could be just as much fun as sailing. There were many things to keep young people occupied on the islands in 1900. Courtesy of John Hutchinson.

(Above) Lucien Moore of Detroit following the boardwalks from the hotel to his cottage. (Below) This picture, titled "seven little rascals," shows what the well-dressed Shoaler was wearing in 1900. Courtesy of John Hutchinson.

Miss Finch, appropriately dressed for the occasion, is waiting to meet the boat at the dock on Appledore. Courtesy of John Hutchinson.

Childe Hassam painting on the porch of Celia Thaxter's cottage. The photograph was probably taken by Karl Thaxter. Courtesy of the Star Island Corporation.

(Above) A typical Celia Thaxter flower arrangement using many vases of various sizes. Photo by Karl Thaxter. Courtesy of the Star Island Corporation. (Below) Mr. Hassam at work on his painting of Alice. Courtesy of John Hutchinson.

Childe Hassam

Frederick Childe Hassam was born in Boston on October 17, 1859. He spent his youth among antiques collected by his father who was a prosperous merchant. Hassam began his art training in Boston under I. M. Gaugengigl and worked for a short period as an illustrator and painter. He spent five years in France studying under Boulanger and Lefebvre and was influenced by Monet. This influence made him one of the leading exponents of American impressionism, or "luminism," as it was called in this country.

Hassam returned from Europe and continued to work as an illustrator and painter. His work was published in such periodicals as *Harpers*, *Scribners*, and *The Century*. Painting was an essential part of his life and he produced an extraordinary number of works that varied in quality because Hassam rarely destroyed an unsuccessful work.

Celia Thaxter had been a pupil of Childe Hassam's in the water color classes that he conducted in Boston in the 1880s. Hassam came to Appledore during the summer of 1890 and the island made a strong impression on him.

A strong affection grew between Hassam and Celia Thaxter and she asked him to illustrate *An Island Garden*. Between 1890 and 1916, Hassam painted the rock forms and the sea that are the dominant features of the landscape. His Appledore pictures usually had a high horizon line and the sky was almost excluded. He painted with noon light that tended to flatten the natural forms and express the stark simplicity of the basic rock and sea motifs. Later Hassam began to include figures in his Appledore paintings.

Most historians agree that Hassam's finest paintings were created in the 1890s. The works that he produced on Appledore over a twenty-year period represent the best examples of American impressionism. He painted *The Room of Flowers*, his view of the Thaxter drawing room that was the site of so many happy gatherings. Celia Thaxter died shortly after its completion. Hassam and fellow painter J. Appleton Brown attended her burial in the family cemetery on a hill behind Celia's cottage. Hassam did not return to the island for several years after the loss of his dear friend.

(Above) Childe Hassam playing dominos with two young ladies. From a private collection. (Below) The artist, the model and the painting in progress. Childe Hassam painting Alice. Courtesy of John Hutchinson.

Childe Hassam playing dominos on Appledore. From a private collection.

(Above, left) Sarah Orne Jewett was a close friend of Celia Thaxter. A talented writer from South Berwick, Maine, Jewett corresponded with Celia on a regular basis. Courtesy of UNH Special Collections. (Above, right) Horace Greeley from an original stereograph by Gurney & Son. Greeley was another well-known figure who was a guest on the Isles of Shoals. Courtesy of the Portsmouth Public Library. (Below, left) Annie Fields, wife of James T. Fields, visited and corresponded regularly with Celia. Courtesy of the Portsmouth Public Library. (Below, right) James T. Fields, the editor of the Atlantic Monthly, *published Celia Thaxter's poems on a regular basis. Courtesy of Rosamond Thaxter.*

William Dean Howells, author, editor, and diplomat, was attracted to the islands which had become a magnet for writers and artists. Courtesy of the Star Island Corporation.

(Above) Celia Thaxter's cottage and garden on Appledore Island. Courtesy of UNH Media Services. (Left) Looking toward Appledore harbor from Celia Thaxter's porch. Photo by Karl Thaxter. Courtesy of the Star Island Corporation.

Celia Thaxter's Garden

Celia Laighton was four years old when she moved to the Isles of Shoals with her parents. At that point in her life, flowers and green grass became a precious sight. A year later, she planted her first garden of marigolds on a small plot that was not more than a square yard in size. Ten years later, Celia moved to Appledore where her father built a hotel and several cottages.

Celia's husband refused to return to the islands after almost losing his life in a boating accident. However, when her parents became older, she felt that she was needed to help with the family business and care for her aging parents, Thomas and Eliza. Income from her writing fueled an independent spirit and she moved into what became known as the Thaxter Cottage on Appledore.

Celia Thaxter planted her famous cutting garden in front of the cottage which is described in her book *An Island Garden*, illustrated in color with the work of American impressionist Childe Hassam. Celia described the 1893 garden in detail, listing 57 varieties of flowers and describing 24 other plants which could be added during the summer season. The flowers decorated her cottage, especially the parlor which had become a salon for the well-known writers, musicians, and artists who summered on the islands.

The re-creation of Celia Thaxter's famous garden has been a project of the Shoals Marine Laboratory which currently occupies the island. At the end of May or early June, 85 trays of flowering plants, prepared by the University of New Hampshire's Thompson School, are shipped out to Appledore. They are planted inside a 15-foot by 50-foot fence which is the site of the original garden. Planting continues throughout the summer and the garden is maintained with the help of area garden clubs and volunteers. Marine laboratory students also help with the planting and weeding which is closely supervised by resident gulls. Green grass and flowers are still a precious sight to all Shoals residents and they are willing to work for their share of Celia's legacy.

Celia Thaxter's garden early in the season. The Appledore Hotel is in the background. From a private collection.

(Above) Appledore tennis courts near Celia's cottage. Courtesy of the Star Island Corporation. (Below) Celia Thaxter in her garden in 1887. Courtesy of Rosamond Thaxter.

Celia Thaxter at age 38. Courtesy of the Portsmouth Public Library.

Eliza Rymes Laighton, the mother of Celia Thaxter. Courtesy of the Star Island Corporation.

The Family Tree

Thomas Laighton (1805–1866)
(Married 1831)
Eliza Rymes (1804–1877)

1. Helen (d. at 11 mos.)
2. Celia (1835–1894)
   (Married 1851)
   Levi Lincoln Thaxter (1821–1884)
   1. Karl (1852–1912)
   2. John (1854–1928)
      (Married 1886)
      Mary Stoddard
      1. Rosamond (1895–1989)
   3. Roland (1858–1932)
      (Married 1886)
      Mabel (Mary) Freeman
      1. Charles Eliot
      2. Katherine
      3. Edmund
      4. Betty
3. Oscar (1839–1939)
4. Cedric (1840–1899)
   (Married 1881)
   Julia Stowell
   1. Margaret
      (Married Edward Forbes)
   2. Barbara
   3. Ruth

(Above) John Thaxter, Celia's second son, was the father of Rosamond. Courtesy of the Star Island Corporation. (Below) The Thaxter farm at Kittery Point, Maine. From a cyanotype. Courtesy of Rosamond Thaxter.

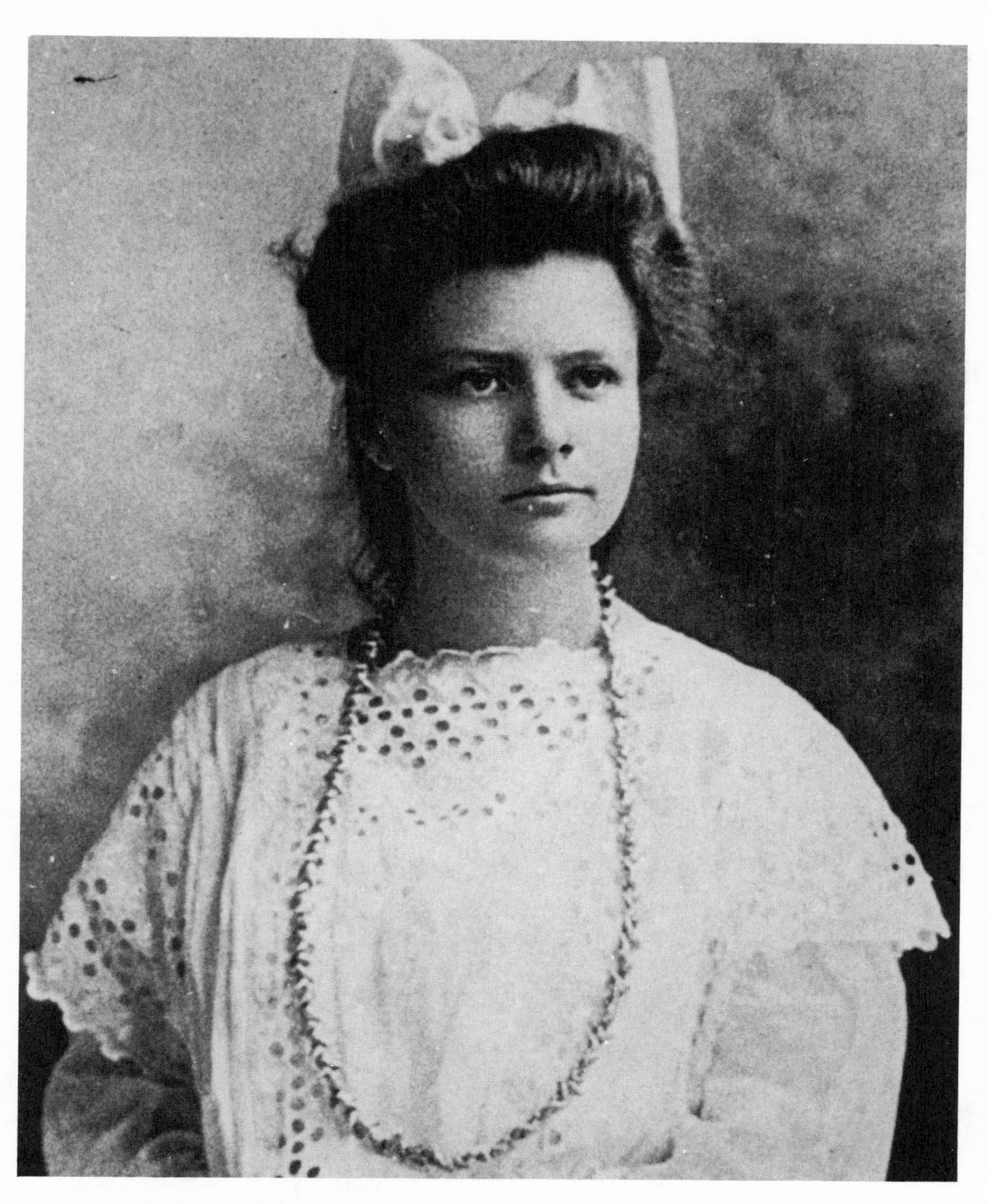

Rosamond Thaxter, John's daughter, at fourteen years of age. From a lantern slide. Courtesy of Portsmouth Public Library.

(Above) Mrs. Roland Thaxter with her four children. Eliot is at the right. Courtesy of the Portsmouth Public Library. (Right) Roland Thaxter, Celia's youngest son who was born in 1858. Photo by Warren's of Boston. Courtesy of the Star Island Corporation.

Cedric Laighton poses for a snapshot on Appledore. c. 1900. Courtesy of John Hutchinson.

(Left) Celia and her two brothers are buried on the island that was their home for so many years. Photo by Gary Samson. (Right) Celia Thaxter's grave marker. She was buried on a little knoll behind her cottage. From a lantern slide. Courtesy of the Portsmouth Public Library.

and has been reprinted many times.

Celia Thaxter, who was in her 59th year, had not been feeling well for some time. On August 25, 1894, friends sent for her son Roland to spend Sunday with her on the island. He found her on the sofa in her parlor with a few close friends. They listened to music and she read a few poems. She retired early accompanied by her personal maid who slept in the room to be available if needed. They awoke at dawn and Celia asked that the curtains be opened so she could see the sunrise. When the maid turned from the window, Celia was dead.

Funeral arrangements were simple. Celia lay in her parlor surrounded by wildflowers and flowers from her garden. Dr. DeNormandie conducted a brief service and her close friends carried her to the gravesite at the top of the hill where her mother and father had been buried. Her burial site was completely covered with green leaves and flowers.

With Celia gone, writers and artists were no longer attracted to Appledore. Five years later Cedric died and Oscar was unable to manage the hotels. He was forced into bankruptcy and continued to live on the island as a guest.

Karl left Appledore after his mother's death. He lived in Portsmouth on a small income provided by Celia and occupied his time with photography. He eventually moved from Portsmouth to Newton to Worcester where he died in 1912.

The Appledore Hotel and all the hotel cottages burned to the ground on September 4, 1914. Small fires were not unusual during the summer season and staff members were trained to deal with them. Unfortunately, only a few people remained on the island late in the season. The crew got the pumps working and nearly had the blaze under control, but a strong southeast wind eventually turned the huge wooden hotel into a roaring inferno. According to some reports, people on the mainland lined the beaches to watch the spectacular fire. Oscar noticed the smoke from Star Island and rowed to the scene of the fire. He rescued a few pictures from Celia's cottage before it was consumed in the blaze. The few remaining cottages were virtually abandoned to vandals and the destructive forces of nature. Blackberry vines and poison ivy closed the paths to all but the muskrats and the birds.

J. Appleton Brown surveying the scene from the porch of the Appledore House. c. 1900. Courtesy of John Hutchinson.

J. Appleton Brown's studio near his cottage on Appledore. Courtesy of John Hutchinson.

J. Appleton Brown

J. Appleton Brown was a frequent visitor to the Isles of Shoals and a close friend of Celia Thaxter's. His delicate paintings and pastels reflected a temperament which his biographer described as "unchangeable in its cheerfulness, very quiet but mighty in the persistence of its flow." Raised in Newburyport and trained in Boston and Paris, Brown's delicate paintings and pastels of apple trees caused him to be called "Appleblossom Brown" by his friends. When financial problems forced Cedric and Oscar to lease plots of land for summer cottages, one was leased to Brown for use as a studio-home.

Brown painted Celia's garden and illustrated her poem "Remonstrance" with the lines: "Come out into the garden, where the crimson phloxes burn."

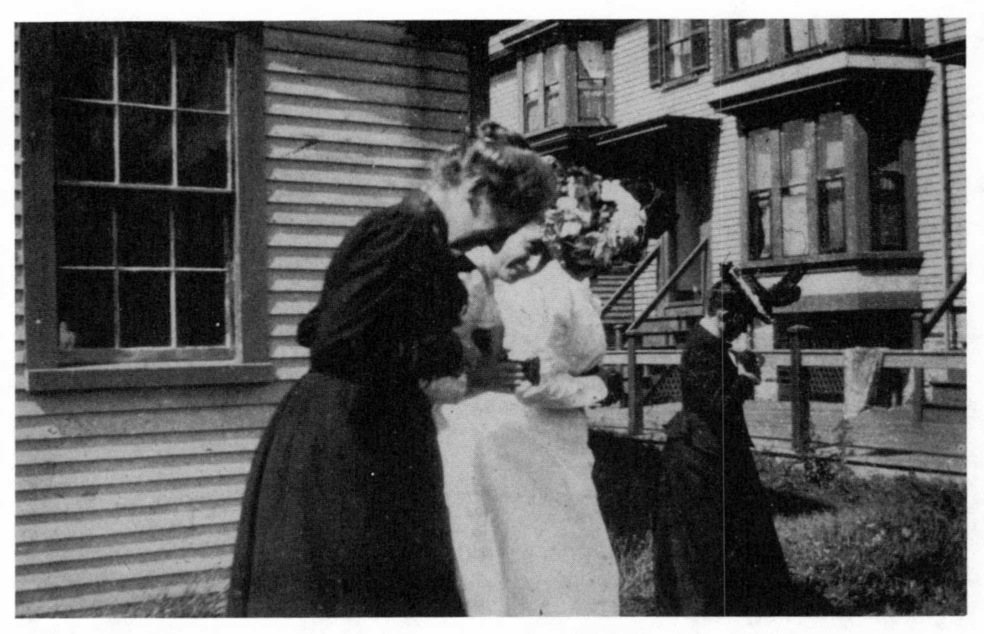

(Above) Mmes. Laighton, Hassam, Foster and Moore photographing on Appledore. c. 1900. (Below) The flag is flying in a stiff breeze over Sunset Pavilion. c. 1900. Courtesy of John Hutchinson.

(Above) This 1908 advertising piece was designed to sell lots on Appledore when the hotel business was no longer profitable. Several of the regular visitors purchased lots but not enough were sold to save the hotels. (Below) The Appledore Hotel and many of the cottages went up in flames after the hotel closed in September, 1914. Courtesy of UNH Media Services.

Celia's son Karl Thaxter posing with one of his friends in March 1904. Courtesy of Rosamond Thaxter.

(Above) The men took time from their busy summer schedules to assist the ladies with their yarn. (Below) The Richter Cottage on Appledore at the turn of the century. Note the board walks that formed a network of paths on the island. Courtesy of John Hutchinson.

Lilla N. Elliott, wife of Thomas H. Elliott, at the turnstile on Star Island. It was Lilla who suggested that they come to the Isles of Shoals rather than attend a church conference at the Weirs in New Hampshire. Elliott arranged with the Laightons to bring the first church conference to the island the following summer. Courtesy of the Portsmouth Public Library.

The Conference Era

MR. AND MRS. THOMAS ELLIOTT of Lowell, Massachusetts, were lay members of the North Middlesex Conference of Unitarian Churches which had its summer meetings at the Weirs on Lake Winnipesaukee. Mr. Elliott was a strong supporter of church conferences, but it was extremely hot at the Weirs in the summer and his wife's health was affected by the heat. In the summer of 1896, Mrs. Elliott suggested that they change their plans and go to the shore where it would be cooler. They changed the tags on their trunks and spent their summer vacation at the Isles of Shoals.

Mr. Elliott enjoyed the islands, but he missed the religious conferences. Noting that both hotels were operating below capacity he discussed the issue with hotel manager Harry Marvin and they made an agreement to hold a conference at the Isles of Shoals. Elliott spent the winter organizing the Isles of Shoals Summer Meetings Association which held its first meeting on Star Island in July, 1897.

The Star Island meetinghouse had been long neglected. The floors were rotted and unsafe, plaster was cracked and dirty, and an opening which had been a door was rough and unplastered. Conference participants accepted the challenge and began to restore the small church. They found the remains of the wooden brackets with three arms in the form of a horizontal cross which were used to hold the lanterns during evening services. Replicas were made and mounted on the inner walls.

Mr. Elliott was determined that the Shoals meetings be free of denominational issues and he invited both Unitarians and Congregationalists to participate in the conferences. Delegates became interested in the history and culture of these unique islands. They watched from the porch as ledge was blasted from Smuttynose and used to build a breakwater between Smuttynose and Cedar. Three years later,

continued on page 129

(Above) Thomas and Lilla Elliott at the Oceanic Hotel in 1910. Photo by Grace Torr. Courtesy of the Star Island Corporation. (Below) Lobby of the second Oceanic Hotel on Star Island. Courtesy of the Portsmouth Public Library.

Unitarian Summer Meetings Association.

ISLES OF SHOALS, N.H.

July 11–18, 1897.

DIRECTIONS FOR THOSE DESIRING TO ATTEND.

First. Send fifty cents, for membership certificate, to T. H. Elliott, Secretary, Lowell, Mass. Send promptly, as accommodations are limited. This certificate ensures the reduced rates of transportation and hotel.

Second. Send names of party, with proper prefix of Mr., Mrs., or Miss to each name, to Mr. H. G. Marvin, Portsmouth, N.H., stating date and exact time for which rooms are required. Rooms will be assigned between July 1 and 10.

Third. Check baggage through to Isles of Shoals, N.H.

Fourth. Go to Portsmouth, N.H., by the Eastern Division of the Boston & Maine, there take steamer "Viking," three or four minutes' walk from station.

STEAMER "VIKING" leaves Portsmouth for Isles of Shoals, 8.00 and 11.20 A.M.; 5.40 P.M.

" " " Star Island for Portsmouth, 6.00, 9.30 A.M., and 3 30 P.M.

Special round-trip tickets will be on sale as follows:—

Good, going, July 10 to July 17, inclusive.

Good, returning, to **July 19**, inclusive, **only**.

Boston,	$2.35
Worcester (via Boston),	3.70
Springfield (via Boston),	5.35
Ayer (via Lowell and Bradford),	2.85
Lowell (via Bradford and Newburyport),	2.35
Lawrence (via Bradford and Newburyport),	1.90
Haverhill (via Georgetown and Newburyport),	1.70
Lynn,	2.00
Salem,	1.85
Newburyport,	1.40
Nashua, N.H. (via Manchester),	2.35
Manchester, N.H.,	1.85
Concord, N.H. (via Manchester),	2.40
Portland, Me.,	2.35

Directions for those attending the Unitarian Summer Meetings in 1897. Courtesy of the Star Island Corporation.

(Above) An interior view of the Star Island meetinghouse after it was restored. The meetinghouse is used regularly by participants at conferences sponsored by the Star Island Corporation. Courtesy of the Portsmouth Public Library. (Below) The Tucke Parsonage and the meetinghouse in 1884. At this time the meetinghouse has a wooden tower. Courtesy of the Star Island Corporation.

(Above) One bag of clubs was used by the golfers on the short Star Island course. Small boys from the hotel are showing great interest in the game. (Below) Three golfers enjoying a short game on Star Island. Notice the sand box by the man's right foot. Sand was used to tee up the ball before wooden tees were invented. Courtesy of John Hutchinson.

Four swimmers and a friend pose on the rocks while attending a Star Island Conference in 1924. Courtesy of the Portsmouth Public Library.

The Fashionable Bathing Costume

Rosamond Thaxter, in her book *Sandpiper*, described the bathing suits worn by the daring young ladies who swam in Babb's Cove during the summer. The ladies used water wings which were blown up each time they went for a swim. Their bathing attire was long black stockings worn beneath a black alpaca bathing suit with baggy bloomers. Over this they wore a skirt which buttoned at the waist and reached the knees. The neckline was high, the short sleeves were puffed, and the outfit was tastefully trimmed with braid.

(Above) This boy in his 1900-period bathing suit is drying off under the watchful eye of his mother in her own bathing costume. Courtesy of John Hutchinson. (Left) Waitress Elizabeth Lindsey of Marblehead, Massachusetts, in her bathing costume, August 5, 1922. Courtesy of the Portsmouth Public Library.

(Above) The large blocks of granite arrived on the William H. Moody *and were unloaded at the dock on Star Island. (Below) One of the six workhorses being unloaded on the island. Courtesy of the New Hampshire Historical Society.*

in 1904, they watched barges with large blocks of granite from Rockport quarries supply the fill for a breakwater between Cedar and Star.

A monument to Captain John Smith was erected in 1884 to honor the famous explorer who first visited the islands in 1614. In poor condition, the monument was replaced in 1914 by the Society of Colonial Wars in New Hampshire.

The Reverend John Tucke monument, to honor a minister who devoted his life to improving conditions on the Isles of Shoals, was also under construction and guests were able to watch the progress of the project. Barges unloaded blocks of granite that were six-foot cubes weighing approximately fifteen tons. A team of six horses pulled the blocks to the site where the monument was being erected. On July 29, 1914, five hundred people came to the island for the dedication of the Tucke monument and the rededication of the Smith monument.

Concern for the future of the islands led delegates to explore the possibility of owning one or more of the islands. When the Appledore Hotel burned in 1914, the movement to acquire Star Island gained momentum. The mortgage on the property was $16,000 and the bank was anxious to unload a high risk property and get their money back into circulation. One other party, an operator of roadhouses, was ready to take over the mortgage and members of the association had to respond quickly or all would be lost.

Lewis Parkhurst, a partner in Ginn and Company, called the Piscataqua Savings Bank, holder of the mortgage, and asked them to send a representative authorized to negotiate and close a sale. He offered $16,000, presented the bank representative with a certified check, and became the new owner of Star Island. He planned to hold the property until the conferees could form a corporation and raise enough money to purchase it from him. In 1916, the Star Island Corporation received its charter. In the meantime a fund raising committee was organized to raise $40,000 to reimburse Mr. Parkhurst, restore the island, acquire a steamboat, and establish an endowment.

On October 15, 1915, donations had reached $13,225. The well-organized campaign reached churches, organizations, and individuals. By April 20, 1916, the fund had reached $45,484.21 and Star Island was now controlled by the Star Island Corporation. They paid $16,000 for the island, spent $6,777 for repairs to the Oceanic Hotel, bought $7,250 worth of stock in the Star Island Steamboat Company, and invested $12,794 in bonds. Improvements included replacing the carpet and wallpaper in the hotel and cottages, painting floors and walls, replacing the plumbing and installing a new sanitation system, contracting for the drilling of an artesian well, and formulating a plan for the future development of the island.

continued on page 149

The granite blocks were unloaded at the dock and placed on a sturdy wagon that moved on a track of wooden planks. Courtesy of the New Hampshire Historical Society.

(Above) A six-horse team pulling the granite blocks over the "railroad" to the site of the Tucke Monument. (Left) The final granite block is being put into place on the Tucke Monument. Courtesy of the New Hampshire Historical Society.

The Tucke Monument on Star Island completed in 1914. Courtesy of the Portsmouth Public Library.

(Above) Star Island after a snowfall in 1914. Note the fence around the Tucke Monument at left and the fence that divided the island with the turnstile in the middle. Courtesy of UNH Media Services. (Below) This picture was labeled "the Five Founders at Star Island." Left to right are Jessie E. Donahue, Oscar Laighton, Millie B. Nichols, and Mr. and Mrs. Thomas Elliott. Courtesy of the Portsmouth Public Library.

A cross marks the location of "Miss Underhill's Chair" on the ledges of Star Island. From a stereograph by the Davis Brothers. Courtesy of the Star Island Corporation.

Tales of Tragedy

Miss Underhill, a Gosport schoolteacher, had a favorite retreat on a high rock on the edge of the ocean where she would go to read and enjoy the view. One day a large wave snatched her from her lofty perch and she was lost in the sea. Postcards now describe the location of her special place as "Miss Underhill's Chair."

"The Choir" standing in front of the well house in front of the Oceanic Hotel. Courtesy of the Portsmouth Public Library.

Captain Perkins of the Sightseer *poses at the dock in 1921. Courtesy of the Star Island Corporation.*

Oscar Laighton was fond of drawing a boat under full sail and adding his autograph to the piece. Courtesy of the Portsmouth Public Library.

Transportation to the Shoals

The opening of one section of the Appledore House in 1848 created a need for regular transportation between Appledore Island and the mainland. Over the years the islands were served by a number of boats including the *Spy*, *Sea Ranger*, *Factory Girl*, *Star of the East*, and steamers *Silver Star*, and *Pioneer*. The *Pioneer* was put into service in 1867, and there was a significant increase in the transient business at the hotel. However, the Laightons' 60-ton yacht *Cecelia* still carried many passengers to Appledore. Sailing to the islands could be a one hour trip if the winds were right. Strong headwinds could stretch the trip to two or three hours or longer if the vessel became becalmed in a gentle swell.

In 1869, the Laightons decided to build a new steamer expressly designed for the run to the Isles of Shoals. It was 100 feet long, had two passenger decks and a 15-by-28-foot paneled cabin. The *Appledore* departed on its maiden voyage on June 25, 1869, carrying several hundred celebrities and paying guests. However, there was still no wharf at Appledore and the last 100 yards had to be negotiated in a row boat. When John Poor built the Oceanic Hotel on Star Island he installed a wharf that offered a "direct landing." The Laightons, who claimed that wharfs would lead to drowning children and wharf rats, had to borrow $15,000 and build a wharf of their own. Poor also purchased a new steamer, *Major*, to compete with the steamer owned by the Laightons. The *Appledore* continued to operate until 1880. At that time the *Major* was acquired by the Laightons and renamed the *Oceanic*.

(Above) Homeward bound. Guests returning from a visit to the islands in 1902. Courtesy of the Portsmouth Public Library. (Below) Ticket to the Isles of Shoals from Portsmouth from the Isles of Shoals Steamship Company. Courtesy of UNH Media Services.

Isles Shoals Steamship Co.

PORTSMOUTH

—TO—

ISLES SHOALS & RETURN

Good on **DATE ISSUE** only

3827

Treas.

GRAHAM & MORSE Managers.

(Above) The steamer Oceanic *arriving at the Star Island dock. The* Pinafore *is the small steamboat leaving the dock. Courtesy of UNH Media Services. (Below) The Oceanic Pier in 1881. Note the water pump in the foreground and the boats at the dock. From the album of Rev. Charles E. Dunn. Courtesy of the Portsmouth Public Library.*

(Above) The steamboat Juliette *coming in to the dock. It was one of the larger steamers to stop at the Isles of Shoals. Courtesy of the Star Island Corporation. (Below) A less-formal group meeting the boat at the Star Island pier. From a lantern slide. Courtesy of the Portsmouth Public Library.*

(Above) The S.S. Sightseer *landing at Star Island in 1929. Courtesy of the Portsmouth Public Library. (Below) The* Sagamore, *under a full head of steam, is leaving for the mainland. Courtesy of UNH Media Services.*

(Above) The Viking *arriving at the dock to bring supplies and new visitors to the island. Courtesy of UNH Media Services. (Below) Two gentlemen are being photographed near their sailing vessel at the Appledore dock. c. 1900. Courtesy of John Hutchinson.*

(Above) The Mineola *on August 30, 1905. The 140-foot steamboat carried 800 passengers and stopped at the Isles of Shoals. Courtesy of Mr. & Mrs. Edward A. Dodd. (Below) The* Kiboko *was used to transport groups between the islands and the mainland from 1946 until 1961. Photo by Lyman Rutledge. Courtesy of the Portsmouth Public Library.*

(Above) The steamboat Stamford *at the Star Island dock. Note the well pump in the foreground and the hay that has been harvested from the front lawn. Courtesy of William Varrell. (Below) The steamboat* Favorite *arriving at the dock. From a stereoview by the Davis Brothers. Courtesy of the Star Island Corporation.*

(Above) The Pink Parlor of the Oceanic Hotel on Star Island was photographed by Lyman Rutledge on August 9, 1924. (Below) This picture of the long dining room at the Oceanic Hotel was also used in a post card and a brochure advertising the virtues of the hotel. Courtesy of the Portsmouth Public Library.

(Above) A 1916 Maypole Dance celebrating the twentieth anniversary of the Unitarian Summer Meetings at the Oceanic Hotel on Star Island. (Below) The barn on Star Island. Courtesy of the Star Island Corporation.

Oceanic

JULY 4,
1906.

Isles of Shoals Fish Chowder.
Mock Turtle Soup.

Baked Bluefish, au Madere. Lobster Cutlets, a la Cardinal.
HOLLANDAISE POTATOES.
Radishes. Cucumbers. Sliced Tomatoes.

Chicken Patties, a la Toulousaise.
Filet of Beef, a la Financiere.
Queen Fritters, Macedoine.

Roast Star Ham, Champagne Sauce.
Plain Lobster Roast Sirloin of Beef, au Jus.
PUNCH, A LA ROMAINE.

Roast Tame Duck, Stuffed, Apple Jelly.

WALDORF SALAD.

Mashed Potatoes. Boiled New Potatoes.
Wax Beans. Green Peas. Succotash.

Young America Cheese. Toasted Crackers.

Apple Pie. Strawberry Shortcake. Lemon Meringue Pie.
Independence Pudding, Liberty Sauce.
Victoria Slice. Banana Ice Cream. Sultana Cake.
Lady Fingers. Africans. Macaroons.

Chilled Watermelon.
Assorted Nuts. Layer Raisins.
CAFE NOIR.

Dinner menu at the Oceanic Hotel on July 4, 1906. Note that "plain lobster" was added as an alternative to the more sophisticated offerings. Courtesy of the Portsmouth Public Library.

(Above) Guests carrying their luggage down to the Star Island boat landing. The second Oceanic Hotel is in the background. This ritual has been repeated many times over the years. Courtesy of UNH Media Services. (Below) A clambake is being organized for the guests near the edge of the Star Island pool. Lobsters, steamed clams, and corn on the cob are basic elements of a New England clambake. Courtesy of the Star Island Corporation.

The Isles of Shoals Congregational Association, organized in 1914, was chartered as the Isles of Shoals Congregational Corporation in 1929. The new status authorized them to hold funds for conferences.

The islands were closed to visitors during the war years of 1917 and 1918. During those years the conferences were held at the Wentworth Hotel in New Castle. However, conferences moved back to Star Island after the war ended and eventually they were expanded from two to ten weeks. Among the new buildings added were Tucke Parsonage in 1927, Parker Hall in 1948, Newton Centre House, Sprague, and Founders cottages in 1953, Baker and YPRU cottages in 1955, and the Vaughan Memorial building in 1960. A new service building was added in 1960, and two converters were installed to purify sea water for use by hotel guests.

In 1924, seven and one half acres of land and three buildings were purchased on Appledore by the Star Island Corporation. In 1929, the Corporation bought all of the remaining vacant land on Appledore giving them control of 95% of the island. The corporation also acquired Duck Island. The rebirth of Appledore Island began in 1928, when the University of New Hampshire leased the three buildings owned by the corporation for a marine zoological laboratory and summer school. The program was directed by Professor C. F. Jackson who purchased another building for his own use. For thirteen years the program grew in numbers and reputation, but was abandoned when the lease ran out and, as a result of World War II, the island became a military base. The concrete observation tower is the remaining memorial of that period.

In 1965, Dr. John M. Kingsbury of Cornell University came to Star Island to participate in a family conference. A specialist in marine algae, he was delighted by the clear, cold water and the wealth of flora and fauna. He developed a plan for a marine science summer program that was enthusiastically supported by representatives of the Star Island Corporation. His immediate plan was to offer a course on Star Island during the two week period in June before the summer conference season began. His ultimate goal was to establish a permanent summer program on Appledore.

Star Island provided living facilities and lecture rooms for the marine science students. In later years, the University of New Hampshire renewed its commitment to the program by providing laboratory space at the Jackson Estuarine Laboratory in Durham. Students spent two weeks on Star Island and two weeks in Durham. The course was very successful and it continued for six more summers. By 1971, when residence on Star Island was extended from two weeks to three, gifts and pledges had reached the level that enabled Dr. Kingsbury to

continued on page 161

(Above) Swimmers in the Star Island pool in August, 1922. There were as many spectators as there were swimmers in this photo by Lyman Rutledge. (Below) Croquet was another form of recreation that was popular on the island. Lyman Rutledge took this photograph in 1924. Courtesy of the Portsmouth Public Library.

Three young women enjoying a marshmallow roast. Courtesy of the Star Island Corporation.

(Above) Softball replaced croquet as the most popular game played on the lawn in front of the Oceanic Hotel. From a lantern slide. (Below) Stone mason Nellis Earl beginning the construction of Parker Hall on Star Island. Courtesy of the Portsmouth Public Library.

(Above) The Newton Centre House under construction in 1951. This was the view from the meetinghouse tower. Courtesy of the Portsmouth Public Library. (Below) Workers pose during the construction of the third Tucke Parsonage in August, 1922. Courtesy of the Portsmouth Public Library.

Oscar Laighton loading his boat for a sightseeing trip around the Isles of Shoals. Courtesy of UNH Media Services.

(Above) The Moore Cottage on Appledore. Courtesy of John Hutchinson. (Below) Oscar Laighton would often draw a codfish on letters or books that he autographed. This is one example of his work. Courtesy of the Portsmouth Public Library.

Professor C. Floyd Jackson who opened a marine zoological laboratory and summer "camp" on Appledore in 1928 and conducted summer classes on the island for fourteen years. Courtesy of UNH Media Services.

(Above) Professor Jackson's marine laboratory program grew in numbers and reputation but it was abandoned at the beginning of World War II. This is his base station on the island. Courtesy of Herb Jackson. (Below) Large fish were of interest to summer Shoalers who were always looking for something to change the routine. This large shark was brought up in a wheelbarrow and parked on the lawn in front of the hotel on Appledore. Courtesy of the Star Island Corporation.

Dr. John M. Kingsbury of Cornell University was the driving force behind the re-establishment of a marine science facility on the Isles of Shoals. Courtesy of George Sylvester.

(Above) The radar tower was left by the military forces when they were removed after World War II. This landmark can be seen from great distances and makes it easy for sailors to identify Appledore. (Below) Hewitt Hall in 1983, when it was being restored to serve as staff quarters for those who worked at the marine lab during the summer. Photo by John D. Bardwell.

The United States Coast Guard occupied this building on Appledore which later became the headquarters for the Shoals Marine Laboratory. Courtesy of the Star Island Corporation.

negotiate a long-term lease of the Star Island Corporation's property on Appledore and begin the construction of the new facilities required for the educational program.

Student volunteers rebuilt the old Coast Guard building and put a new roof on one of the more substantial old buildings. A landing was built, roads were cut, and a utility building was constructed. In 1972, Kiggins Commons was built and other structures were renovated. The classes moved to Appledore in 1973. Called the Shoals Marine Laboratory, it was operated by Cornell University in cooperation with the University of New Hampshire. The two institutions provided members of the core faculty and shared the responsibility for course offerings. The physical plant grew to include nine buildings. The Palmer-Kinne Laboratory provided space for sixty students, there were three new dormitories, and renovated structures provided space for academic and operating staff, a library, infirmary, and office.

On November 27, 1973, Governor Meldrim Thomson held a press conference in Concord, New Hampshire, to announce plans for Olympic Refineries to locate in New Hampshire. Olympic had already obtained firm purchase options for several thousand acres on Durham Point, and was prepared to invest $600 million to build a 400,000 barrel per day oil refinery in that area. The largest oil refinery ever built from scratch anywhere in the world was being proposed by a Monaco-based firm that had never before built an oil refinery.

Since early September, three teams of realtors had been buying options on land in Rye, Portsmouth, and Dover to be used a "hunting preserve" or for "conservation purposes." They paid $6 million for options on 3,500 acres in Durham, an acreage that represented 25% of the total land area of the town. They optioned 700 acres in Portsmouth for pipelines and terminals and a large swath across Rye to the shore at Concord Point.

Olympic Refineries was being financed by Aristotle Onassis who planned to bring light crude oil from Saudi Arabia in his supertankers. They would offload at a monobuoy or a fixed dock in the lee of the Isles of Shoals. Some of the oil would be trans-shipped in smaller tankers to other east coast locations. The balance would flow through an underwater pipeline to the refinery in Durham which would be operating by 1976. Each of the Onassis supertankers, which was as large or larger than two of the three New Hampshire islands, was owned by a separate holding company. One such company was dissolved two days after the *Olympic Arrow* went aground and caused a major oil spill in Nova Scotia. The new facilities at the Shoals Marine Laboratory would be useless if there was even a minor oil spill near the islands.

Officers of the Star Island Corporation refused an offer of $1 mil-

continued on page 169

(Above) The Grass Foundation Laboratory was one of the first buildings constructed as part of the marine laboratory building program. It houses the generators which provide electricity for the island. Photo by John D. Bardwell. (Below) A view of the marine lab site just after the completion of Kiggins Commons in 1977. The building at left has been razed but the two cottages on the right (Hewitt Hall and Hamilton House) have been completely restored. Photo by Gary Samson.

(Above) An orientation session taking place on the porch of Kiggins Commons. Courtesy of George Sylvester. (Below) A new dormitory at the Shoals Marine Laboratory in 1983. The gulls have already established residence there. Photo by John D. Bardwell.

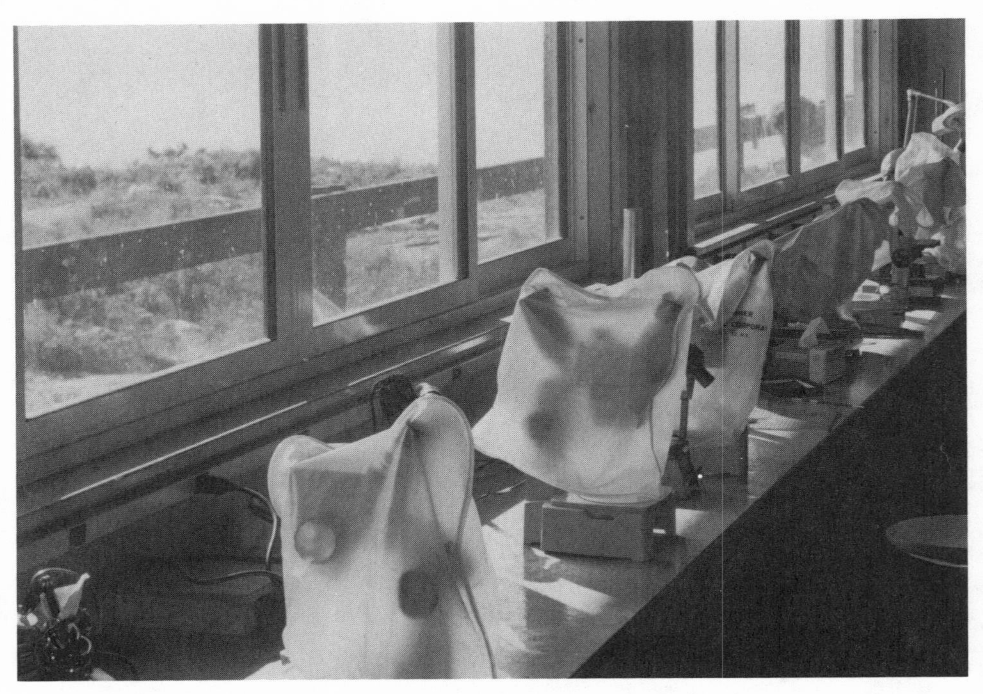

(Above) Microscopes are lined up on the counter in the Palmer-Kinne Lab. Photo by John D. Bardwell. (Below) Students examine a tray filled with sea plants gathered along the rocky shore. Courtesy of UNH Media Services.

(Above) The UNH research vessel Jere Chase *moving up into Babb's Cove near the Appledore dock. (Below) Two students dissecting a seastar during a marine biology class in Palmer-Kinne Laboratory. Courtesy of UNH Media Services.*

(Above) A marine science class being briefed before boarding the Jere Chase *for an instructional session on the research vessel. Courtesy of UNH Media Services. (Below) Rosamond Thaxter, granddaughter of Celia Thaxter, built this shelter which she used when she was on the island of Smuttynose. The door was never locked and visitors were welcome to use it. Photo by John D. Bardwell.*

The Samuel Haley house on Smuttynose is considered to be one of the oldest houses in Maine. This is how it appeared in 1983. Photo by John D. Bardwell.

(Above) The building on Lunging Island was also known as "the honeymoon cottage," and this is how it appeared after it was restored. From an original lantern slide. Courtesy of the Portsmouth Public Library. (Below) Oscar Laighton standing in front of his house on Lunging Island. The property was later sold to Rev. Frank Crandall. Courtesy of the Star Island Corporation.

lion to sell the island to Olympic Refineries. Rosamond Thaxter said, "Over my dead body will they get Smuttynose." The lobstermen on Cedar and Appledore were opposed to the plan and the Maine Historic Preservation Commission moved quickly to put the Maine islands on the National Register of Historic Places. The taxes on Lunging Island were increased from $74 to $1,043.00 although the Randalls received few services from the town of Rye. Their taxes were eventually reduced to $643 but they were "set up" for eminent domain proceedings so they accepted Olympic's generous offer for an option to purchase their precious island.

Olympic's public information meetings were badly staged and they gained little support for the proposal. Aristotle Onassis announced that the refinery would be "as clean as a clinic without smoke or smell." He offered to fund a pollution research laboratory at the University of New Hampshire which had refused to participate in a poll of faculty, staff, and students to determine if they supported the refinery. Five state legislators suggested that they would not support any expansion of the UNH physical plant that would use additional energy if the poll indicated that the majority opposed the refinery.

The Olympic plan began to unravel on December 21, 1973, when Dudley Dudley introduced House Bill 18: *An act requiring local approval prior to approval of site plans for oil refineries.*

Local action was swift and decisive. On March 5, 1974, the Shoals Marine Laboratory announced that it would cease all construction until the question was settled. Newmarket voted 523 to 401 to locate an oil refinery *in Durham*. Eighty-seven percent of the Rye voters supported an ordinance that restricted Lunging Island to single family housing. On March 6, 1974, Durham voted 1,254 to 144 against rezoning the town to facilitate the Olympic proposal. However, the fact that 90% of the voters were against the refinery in their town was not enough for Governor Thomson who commented that the results were "unimpressive."

On March 7th, the Roberts bill rejecting local control over oil refineries was itself rejected by a 233 to 109 vote of the New Hampshire Legislature. Dudley Dudley's bill making local approval mandatory was approved by a voice vote.

The issue became one of local control and was decided by Durham voters who were against having an oil refinery in their college community. Aristotle Onassis and his supertankers would not be off-loading in the unpolluted waters near the Isles of Shoals, and Lunging Island would not be the site of a pumping station.

Aristotle Onassis once said, "You don't force with money, you seduce with it."

Thomas H. Elliott once said, "The Islands always rise to the occasion."

Arthur Borror, associate director of the Shoals Marine Laboratory, teacher of zoology and well known ornithologist. Courtesy of UNH Media Services.

(Above) J. B. Heiser, director of the Shoals Marine Laboratory, following up on an administrative matter requiring his serious attention. Courtesy of George Sylvester. (Below) Instructional sessions take place "in the field" at the Shoals Marine Laboratory. Courtesy of George Sylvester.

(Above) The truck is unloaded from the Kingsbury *after being carried from the mainland. (Below) Students of marine biology conducting studies aboard the "floating lab." Courtesy of UNH Media Services.*

The old Coast Guard building on Appledore was converted for use by the Shoals Marine Laboratory staff. This is how it appeared in July, 1983. Photo by John D. Bardwell.

A view of the old Appledore dock through the vines at the Laighton cottage. Courtesy of John Hutchinson.

Epilogue

ALTHOUGH THE ISLES OF SHOALS are small in area, barren in appearance, and have a severe winter climate, James Garvin noted on the National Register nomination form that they have "exerted an historical and cultural influence that is disproportionate with their modest area and resources." Strategically located in the southern part of the Gulf of Maine, the Shoals first were recognized during the early seventeenth century as an important defensive outpost and as a fishing depot of inestimable value.

Today, lobster boats and recreational fishing boats still operate off the Shoals, but the rocky islands, their tidal margins, and the waters that surround them possess an unspoiled marine environment of great scientific value. They provide a habitat for many species of marine animal life. Two species of gulls, black-crowned night herons, double-crested cormorants, snowy egrets, glossy ibis, and black guillemots all nest at the Shoals, and for some of these species this represents the extreme limit of their nesting range in North America. A checklist of marine flora and fauna compiled by the staff of the Shoals Marine Laboratory in 1989 included 505 species of invertebrates, 198 species of algae, 63 species of fish, and 274 species of birds, including those seen at sea east of the islands and observed on the islands during migration. The Isles of Shoals is now listed as a New England Natural Area, and Duck Island, which is owned by the Star Island Corporation, has been set aside for conservation purposes under the supervision of the Shoals Marine Laboratory. The entire archipelago is utilized for intensive studies in marine biology by Cornell University and the University of New Hampshire, through the Shoals Marine Laboratory.

Botanically, the Isles of Shoals are characterized by sparse and

continued on page 181

The crew of the UNH research vessel Jere Chase *assisting a diver with his gear. Courtesy of UNH Media Services.*

(Above) A rubber boat takes the research team to the dive site. Courtesy of UNH Media Services. (Below) Three immature gulls watching for their harried parents to return with more food. Courtesy of UNH Media Services.

(Above) Two veteran Shoalers relaxing on the porch of one of the dorms at the marine laboratory. (Below) Students assembled on the rocks near the dock waiting for the arrival of the research vessel. Courtesy of UNH Media Services.

A bird study session on the porch of the Palmer-Kinne Laboratory at the Shoals Marine Laboratory. Courtesy of UNH Media Services.

(Above) A view of Star Island across Gosport Harbor from Smuttynose. (Below) Hamilton House is another restored cottage that now contains the main lecture hall and the island office for the Marine Lab. This is how it appeared in 1983. Photos by John D. Bardwell.

hardy vegetation with few trees. Essentially all of the soil is post-glacial, and the thin soil and cold winter winds have prevented the development of substantial numbers of woody plants. Nevertheless, more than 250 land plant species have been identified on the islands.

The Shoals Marine Laboratory opens each summer to offer basic credit courses in field marine science primarily for undergraduate students. Most marine laboratories are open primarily to graduate students, so these courses provide an opportunity for younger scholars to explore an interest in marine science. A variety of short non-credit courses is open to the public. The physical facilities include 10 new or renovated buildings, salt and fresh water systems, a sewerage disposal system, an electrical generating system, and a number of boats. The *R. V. John M. Kingsbury* is the pride of the fleet and was designed to meet the needs of educators and marine researchers at the laboratory.

The Star Island Conference Center has survived two wars, hurricanes, and a series of financial crises to emerge as a popular location for summer religious conferences. Since 1916, under the stewardship of the Corporation, the islands have been protected from commercial development. The physical environment remains conducive to religious and philosophical contemplation and to scientific field research. In 1988, Star Island hosted fifteen conferences during the twelve weeks between June 17 and September 9. The registration in every conference was close to capacity, and it is reasonable to expect that they will continue into the indefinite future. Religious Education and International Affairs are the oldest conferences of the summer meetings. The Religious Education program was first offered in 1908 by the Unitarian Sunday School Union and was attended by those who wanted to improve their teaching. Family conferences are well attended, bringing financial stability and children who grow to love the island. The children become potential participants in future conferences. And best of all, the wonderful old Oceanic Hotel is now equipped with an automatic sprinkler system which helps to insure that the antique structure will continue to be the center of conference activity for many years to come.

The young employees of the Star Island Conference Center are known as Pelicans. In addition to their regular duties, they are expected to entertain on special occasions. Virginia McGill wrote the words to one of their musical routines that contained the following lines:

We'll come back, you will come back,
There's no question whatsoever,
Shoals memories live forever,
We'll always get together.

Bibliography

Books

Boden, Gary T. *The Vascular Flora of Appledore Island*. Ithaca, New York: The Shoals Marine Laboratory, 1977.

Borror, Arthur C. *Breeding Birds of the Isles of Shoals: with Special Reference to Appledore Island*. Ithaca, New York: The Shoals Marine Laboratory, 1980.

Caldwell, Bill. *Islands of Maine: Where America Really Began*. Portland, Maine: Guy Gannett Publishing Company, 1981.

Carter, Robert. *Carter's Coast of New England*. Somersworth, New Hampshire: The New Hampshire Publishing Company, 1969.

Clark, Charles E. *The Eastern Frontier*. New York: Alfred A. Knopf, 1970.

Cook, Fred J. *Privateers of '76*. New York: The Bobbs-Merrill Company, Inc., 1976.

Cornish, Louis C. *The Story of the Isles of Shoals*. Boston: The Beacon Press, 1936.

Deane, John. *A Narrative of the Shipwreck of the Nottingham Galley*. Portland, Maine: The Provincial Press, 1968. (Reprint of the original published in 1711.)

Drake, Samuel Adams. *Nooks and Corners of the New England Coast*. New York: Harper & Brothers, 1875.

Faxon, Susan, ed. *A Stern and Lovely Scene*. Boston: The Nimrod Press, 1978.

Fields, Annie, and Rose Lamb, eds. *Letters of Celia Thaxter*. Boston and New York: Houghton, Mifflin and Company, 1895.

Fowler-Billings, Katherine. *Geology of the Isles of Shoals*. Concord, New Hampshire: State Planning and Development Commission, 1959.

Frost, Joseph W. P. *Sir William Pepperrell, Bart. (1696–1759) His Britannic Majesty's Obedient Servant of Piscataqua*. New York: The Newcomen Society in North America, 1951.

Gibbs, Jane M. *Whales Off New England*. Newbury, Massachusetts: Gibbs & Gibbs, 1982.

Griffith, Fuller. *The Lithographs of Childe Hassam: A Catalog*. New York: Martin Gordon Inc., 1980.

Hammond, Otis Grant, ed. *Dedication of a Memorial to Reverend John Tucke: 1702–1773*. Concord, New Hampshire: The New Hampshire Historical Society, 1914.

Hay, John, and Peter Farb. *The Atlantic Shore: Human and Natural History from Long Island to Labrador*. New York and London: Harper & Row Publishers, 1966.

Hoopes, Donelson F. *Childe Hassam*. New York: Watson-Guptill Publications, 1988.

Howard, Richard A. *Flowers of Star Island, the Isles of Shoals*. Jamaica Plain, Massachusetts: The Arnold Arboretum, 1968.

Jager, Ronald, and Grace Jager. *New Hampshire, An Illustrated History of the Granite State*. Woodland Hills, California: Windsor Publications Inc., 1983.

Jenness, John Scribner. *The Isles of Shoals: An Historic Sketch*. New York: Hurd and Houghton, 1875.

Keatts, Henry. *New England's Legacy of Shipwrecks*. Kings Point, New York: American Merchant Marine Museum Press, 1988.

Kingsbury, John M. *Oil and Water: The New Hampshire Story*. Ithaca, New

York: The Shoals Marine Laboratory, 1975.

Laighton, Oscar. *Ninety Years at the Isles of Shoals*. Boston: The Beacon Press, 1930.

———. *Songs and Sonnets*. Privately Printed.

———. *Songs from Appledore*. Privately Printed, 1899.

McGill, Frederick T., Jr., ed. *Letters to Celia: Written during the years 1860–1875 to Celia Laighton Thaxter by her brother Cedric Laighton*. Boston: The Star Island Corporation, 1972.

McGill, Frederick T., Jr., and Virginia F. McGill. *Something Like a Star*. Boston: The Star Island Corporation, 1989.

Molloy, Anne. *Celia's Lighthouse*. Boston: Houghton Mifflin Company, 1949.

Montegeu, M. Tzl. *Ancient and Modern Isles of Shoals from their Discovery to the Present Time*. Boston: G. Alex. Emery, 1872.

Portsmouth Naval Shipyard. *Cradle of American Shipbuilding*. Portsmouth, N.H., 1978.

Penrose, Charles. *They Live on a Rock in the Sea: The Isles of Shoals in Colonial Days*. New York: The Newcomen Society in North America, 1957.

Randall, Peter E. *All Creation and the Isles of Shoals*. Camden, Maine: Down East Books, 1980.

Roberts, Kenneth. *Boon Island*. Garden City, New York: Doubleday & Company, Inc., 1956.

———. *The Lively Lady*. Garden City, New York: Doubleday Doran & Company, Inc., 1933.

Rolde, Neil. *Sir William Pepperrell of Colonial New England*. Brunswick, Maine: The Harpswell Press, 1982.

Rutledge, Lyman V. *Midnight Murder at Smuttynose*. Boston: The Starr King Press, 1958.

———. *Ten Miles Out*. Sixth Edition. Portsmouth, New Hampshire: Peter E. Randall Publisher, 1984.

———. *The Isles of Shoals in Lore and Legend*. Boston: The Star Island Corporation, 1971.

Snow, Edward Rowe. *Famous New England Lighthouses*. Boston: The Yankee Publishing Company, 1945.

———. *The Lighthouses of New England: 1716–1973*. New York: Dodd, Mead & Company, 1973.

———. *Pirates and Buccaneers of the Atlantic Coast*. Boston: The Yankee Publishing Company, 1944.

———. *Pirates, Shipwrecks and Historic Chronicles*. New York: Dodd, Mead & Company, 1981.

———. *True Tales of Buried Treasure*. New York: Dodd, Mead & Company, 1952.

Sylvester, Herbert Milton. *Ye Romance of Old York*. Boston: Stanhope Press, 1906.

Thaxter, Celia. "A Memorable Murder," in *Stories by American Authors*. New York: Charles Scribner's Sons, 1885.

———. *Among the Isles of Shoals*. Boston: J. R. Osgood & Company, 1873.

———. *An Island Garden*. Bowie, Maryland: Heritage Books Inc., 1978.

———. *The Heavenly Guest*. Andover, Massachusetts: Smith & Coutts Co., 1835.

———. *Poems for Children*. Boston: Houghton, Mifflin and Company, 1884.

———. *Representative Poems*. Boston: The Star Island Corporation, 1977.

Thaxter, Rosamond. *Sandpiper: The Life & Letters of Celia Thaxter and Her Home on the Isles of Shoals, her Family, Friends & Favorite Poems*. Francestown, New Hampshire: The Marshall Jones Company, 1963.

Vallier, Jane E. *Poet on Demand*. Camden, Maine: Down East Books, 1982.

Varrell, William M. *Summer by-the-sea: The Golden Era of Victorian Beach Resorts*. Portsmouth, New Hampshire: The Strawberry Bank Print Shop, 1972.

Winslow, Richard E., III. *Portsmouth-Built: Submarines of the Portsmouth Naval Shipyard*. Portsmouth, New Hampshire: Peter E. Randall Publisher, 1985.

———. *Wealth and Honour: Portsmouth During the Golden Age of Privateering, 1775–1815*. Portsmouth, New Hampshire: Peter E. Randall Publisher, 1988.

Articles, Maps and Papers

Farrell, Robert T., and Faith Harrington. "The Shoals Nautical Archaeological Project (SNAP), Isles of Shoals, Maine/New Hampshire, USA." *The International Journal of Nautical Archaeology and Underwater Exploration*, Vol. 16, No. 4, 1987.

Garvin, James L. "The Isles of Shoals." *National Register of Historic Places Inventory-Nomination Form*, for the Maine Historic Preservation Commission. February 26, 1974. Revised, September, 1979.

Harrington, Faith. "Archaeology at the Isles of Shoals." *Context*, Vol. 6, No. 3–4, Spring 1988.

———. "Field Report Isles of Shoals Archaeological Project Summer 1987." Draft. October 23, 1987.

———. "Historic Archaeology Field School at the Isles of Shoals." *The New Hampshire Archeological Society Newsletter*, Vol. 4, No. 1, Spring 1988.

———. "Threads of History at the Shoals." *The Appledore Times*. The Shoals Marine Laboratory, Spring 1988.

Harrington, Faith, and Victoria B. Kenyon. "New Hampshire Coastal Sites Survey, Summer 1986." *The New Hampshire Archaeologist*, Vol. 28, No. 1, 1984.

McClure, Andrew. "Open Horizon." *New Hampshire Profiles*, Vol. 37, No. 9, September 1988.

Moore, R. W. "You Will Return: Appledore Island Calls Alumni Back." 1988.

"Save 20 in Wreck Off Isle of Shoals." *Portsmouth Herald*, Portsmouth, New Hampshire, February 11, 1944.

Shurtleff, Elizabeth. “Map of the Isles of Shoals formerly known as Smiths Iles.” 1927.

Sylvester, George A. “Appledore Sampler: The Shoals Marine Laboratory Explained and Visitor’s Guide to Survival.” An unpublished paper which began as a Christmas letter to friends and just grew from there. It is currently stored in the memory of his computer.

Tallman, Louise H. “A Week At Star Island.” Unpublished report of archaeological studies, September 19–25, 1988.

Ulinski, Mary. “A Trip to Celia Thaxter’s Garden on the Isles of Shoals.” *Foster’s Daily Democrat*, Dover, New Hampshire, September 1, 1988.

Webber, Samuell, and George Jacob. “Appraisal of Mr. John Stover’s Shallop.” *Documentary History of the State of Maine*, an oath and written appraisal recorded on May 23, 1711, by Abraham Preble, Justice of the Peace.

Index

Note: Numerals in italics indicate an illustration of the subject mentioned.

About the Author

John D. Bardwell, director of Media Services at the University of New Hampshire, is a 1955 graduate of UNH.

Publications include *The Diary of the Portsmouth, Kittery and York Electric Railroad, A History of the Country Club at York, Maine,* and he is co-author of *Images of a University: A Photographic History of the University of New Hampshire, The White Mountains of New Hampshire: A Visual History* and *The Lakes Region of New Hampshire: A Visual History.*

Mr. Bardwell is a member of the Piscataqua Pioneers, the Society of Colonial Wars, the New Hampshire Archaeological Society, the Maine Citizens for Historic Preservation, the Old York Historical Society and is a Proprietor of the Portsmouth Athenaeum. In 1979, he received the State of Maine Historic Preservation Award for his contributions to the state preservation program.

The author has degrees from UNH, Boston University, and the University of Southern Maine. He did advanced graduate work at Indiana University. Mr. Bardwell and his wife Anne live in York, Maine, with their two children, Melissa and Dwight. Melissa is a student at the University of Southern Maine and Dwight attends the University of New Hampshire.